Allies in Wartime

The Alaska-Siberia Airway During World War II

Whereas the Governments of the United States of America and the Union of Soviet Socialist Republics declare that they are engaged in a cooperative undertaking, together with every other nation or people of like mind, to the end of laying the bases of a just and enduring world peace securing order under law to themselves and all nations...

— **Washington, D.C., June 11, 1942**

Edited by

Alexander B. Dolitsky

Published by
Alaska-Siberia Research Center
P.O. Box 34871
Juneau, Alaska 99803
Publication No. 13

www.aksrc.org

Copyright © 2007 by the Alaska-Siberia Research Center (AKSRC)

First Edition

Front Cover: *WWII Alaska-Siberia Lend-Lease Memorial, Fairbanks, Alaska,* © *AKSRC 2006. Project of the Alaska-Siberia Research Center; www.aksrc.org; 907-789-3854. Project Manager: Alexander B. Dolitsky. Photo by Richard T. Wallen, Sculptor.*

Back Cover: *Women Airforce Service Pilots (WASP) Shirley Slade on the cover of* Life *magazine, July 19, 1943.* Life® *used by permission of* Life, *Inc. The war poster, "Do the job he left behind," courtesy of the University of Minnesota Libraries, Manuscripts Division.*

Printed and bound by Amica, Inc., Kent, WA, U.S.A.
Printed in China

General Editor and Production Manager: *Alexander B. Dolitsky*
General Copy Editor: *Liz Dodd, IDTC*
Copy Editor: *Kathy Kolkhorst Ruddy*
Consultants/Historians: *Ilya Grinberg, Blake Smith, William Ruddy, Robert Price*
Cartographer: *Brad Slama, Slama Design, Inc.*
Book designer: *Matt Knutson, InterDesign*

©Alaska-Siberia Research Center (AKSRC) 2007

Hardback edition ISBN 978-0-9653891-6-7
Keywords: Alaska, Siberia, Alaska-Siberia Airway, Allies, World War II, WASP

The paper in this book meets the guidelines for permanence and durability of the Committee on Production Guidelines for Book Longevity of the Council on Library Resources.

THE STRUCTURE OF WORLD PEACE CANNOT BE THE WORK OF ONE MAN, OR ONE PARTY, OR ONE NATION…IT MUST BE A PEACE WHICH RESTS ON THE COOPERATIVE EFFORT OF THE WHOLE WORLD.

— Franklin Delano Roosevelt, March 1, 1945
Address to Congress on the Yalta Conference

Table of Contents

The Alaska-Siberia Airway: From the Home Front to the Front Lines

Celebrating the Home Front in Fairbanks

Transliteration Table

The system of transliteration adopted in this work is that of the United States Board of Geographic Names, with slight modifications for technical reasons. Instead of **e**, we use **ye** at the beginning of names, after vowels and after the soft sign (**ь**), or **yo** (**ё**) where **e** is accented as **ё**. The soft sign (**ь**) and hard sign (**ъ**) have no sound value but they soften or harden the sound of the letter in front of them. A hard sign (**ъ**) is transliterated when in the middle of a word and disregarded when final.

Russian Letters		Transliteration	
А	*а*	a	(as in star, car, Arkansas)
Б	*б*	b	(as in boots, Bill, Britain)
В	*в*	v	(as in voice, Virginia)
Г	*г*	g	(as in go, good, Michigan)
Д	*д*	d	(as in do, road, Dakota)
Е	*е*	ye	(as in met, yes)
Ё	*ё*	yo	(as in yonder, York)
Ж	*ж*	zh	(as in pleasure)
З	*з*	z	(as in zoo, is, Kansas)
И	*и*	i	(as in meet, seat)
Й	*й*	y	(as in may, boy)
К	*к*	k	(as in cat, kind, Kentucky)
Л	*л*	l	(as in belt, lion, Florida)
М	*м*	m	(as in amuse, mother, Mexico)
Н	*н*	n	(as in now, noose, Nebraska)
О	*о*	o	(as in port, comb, Oklahoma)
П	*п*	p	(as in pure, poor, Portland)
Р	*р*	r	(as in river, trilled, Arizona)
С	*с*	s	(as in swim, SOS, South)
Т	*т*	t	(as in stool, tiger, Texas)
У	*у*	u	(as in lunar, tune)
Ф	*ф*	f	(as in food, funny, California)
Х	*х*	kh	(as in Loch Ness)
Ц	*ц*	ts	(as in its, quartz, waltz)
Ч	*ч*	ch	(as in cheap, chain, cheese)
Ш	*ш*	sh	(as in fish, sheep, shrimp)
Щ	*щ*	shch	(as in borsch)
Ъ	*ъ*	"	(hard sign; no equivalent)
Ы	*ы*	y	(as in rip, flip)
Ь	*ь*	'	(soft sign; no equivalent)
Э	*э*	e	(as in best, chest, effort)
Ю	*ю*	yu	(as in you, Yukon)
Я	*я*	ya	(as in yard, yahoo)

The Contributors

John Binkley is a former Alaska State Senator from Fairbanks, Alaska, U.S.A.

Peter Broom is the United Kingdom Deputy Consul General, San Francisco, California. U.K.

Frederic Desagneaux is the French Consul General, San Francisco, California. France.

Alexander B. Dolitsky is the Chairman/Project Manager of the Alaska-Siberia Research Center, Juneau, Alaska, U.S.A.

Sergei B. Ivanov is the Russian Minister of Defense and Deputy of the Russian Government, Moscow, Russia.

Rick Findley is the Lieutenant General, Deputy Commander of the North American Aerospace Defense Command, Canada.

Jeffrey W. Hahn is a Professor of Political Science, Villanova University, Villanova, Pennsylvania, U.S.A.

Robert Huber is the President of the National Council for Eurasian and East European Research, Seattle, Washington, U.S.A.

Miriam J. Lancaster is a Captain (Ret.) of the United States Public Health Service, and a member of the Board of Directors of the Alaska-Siberia Research Center, Stanwood, Washington, U.S.A.

Loren Leman is the Lieutenant Governor of the State of Alaska, U.S.A.

Karen Matthias is the Canadian Consul, Anchorage, Alaska. Canada.

Frank H. Murkowski is a former United States Senator and the Governor of Alaska, U.S.A.

Ivan E. Negenblya is a Civil Aviation Engineer, author, and historian, Yakutsk, Sacha Republic, Russia.

Wallace M. Olson is a Professor of Anthropology (Emeritus), University of Alaska Southeast, Juneau, Alaska, U.S.A.

William G. Ruddy is an attorney and President of the Alaska-Siberia Research Center, Juneau, Alaska, U.S.A.

Donald H. Rumsfeld is the U.S. Secretary of Defense, Washington, D.C., U.S.A.

Blake W. Smith is a recreational pilot, author, and historian, Surrey, British Columbia, Canada.

Ted Stevens is a United States Senator for Alaska, U.S.A.

Yuri V. Ushakov is the Russian Ambassador to the United States, Washington, D.C. Russia.

Gary Wilken is an Alaska State Senator from Fairbanks, Alaska, U.S.A.

Acknowledgments

My first interview of an Alaska-Siberia Lend-Lease Airway participant took place with Bill Schoeppe, on January 17, 1993. Schoeppe, who has since passed away, was a certified aircraft mechanic who in World War II had been stationed in Fairbanks and Nome from 1942 to 1945, and in the Aleutians in 1945.

In the winter of 1993, Mr. Schoeppe, who had learned of my interest in the history of the World War II Alaska-Siberia (ALSIB) Lend-Lease program, invited me to his home in Juneau for a conversation and a cup of tea. During our initial talk, Bill had much to say about his wartime experiences in Fairbanks, Nome, and the Aleutians, and over the ensuing months he and I would meet many times; each conversation revealing another exciting recollection about this dramatic time in Alaska's history. Two years after our first meeting, Bill asked me in one of his letters, "Mr. Dolitsky, do you know if there is any memorial in Fairbanks regarding the 1942-1945 Russian-U.S. Lend-Lease?"[1] The answer at the time was "No," but Bill's question inspired me to pursue the subject, and led to the initiation of the WWII Alaska-Siberia Lend-Lease Memorial Project for Fairbanks, and, ultimately, to this publication.

Bill Schoeppe would be pleased to know that on August 27th, 2006, the Alaska-Siberia Research Center, through the hard work of its board members and others, fulfilled his dream and that of other veterans of the ALSIB program by erecting the World War II Lend-Lease Memorial in Fairbanks, as a permanent reminder to present and future generations of the heroism and sacrifices of American and Soviet ALSIB participants. I am sincerely grateful to Bill Schoeppe, a modest and thoughtful mechanic in Alaska during the war, for his dedication and hard work through which he contributed to the victory of peace-seeking nations over Nazi Germany and the Axis powers.

I am thankful to many WWII veterans and participants of the ALSIB program — my father Boris Dolitsky (Soviet Army Officer from 1939 to 1947), Ginny Wood (Women Airforce Service Pilots, WASP), Ellen Campbell (WASP), Celia Hunter (WASP), Randy Acord (test pilot), Charles Binkley (riverboat captain), James Miller (ALSIB ferry pilot), Jess Hall (ALSIB ferry pilot), Pat Carothers (WWII veteran), and Gerald Dorsher (Veteran of Foreign Wars) — all of whom have provided invaluable information and historic recollections of the war for various ALSIB projects, and for this book in particular.

The ALSIB projects, including this publication, would not be possible without the support and contributions of the Board Members of the Alaska-Siberia Research Center: William Ruddy, Robert Price, John Binkley, Dr. Anna Kerttula, Dr. Jeffrey Hahn, Miriam Lancaster, and Mead Treadwell.

I am also thankful to the distinguished writers who contributed to this work, and to book designer Matt Knutson, cartographer Brad Slama, copy editors Liz Dodd, Kathy Kolkhorst Ruddy and Miriam Lancaster, and consultant/historian Ilya Grinberg of the Buffalo State University at Niagara Falls, NY, for their hard work, unique expertise, interest in the project, and valuable insights that led this publication to its ultimate success.

Alexander B. Dolitsky
Chairman/Project Manager
Alaska-Siberia Research Center
Juneau, Alaska

---

[1] Written correspondence with Bill Schoeppe, dated 07/12/95, Dolitsky's private collection.

Preface I

This book is a collection of articles, essays and speeches that together illuminate a remarkable chapter in human history: the Alaska-Siberia Airway during World War II. The distinguished writers found herein include well-known historians, anthropologists, diplomats, and political leaders representing the United States, Russia, Great Britain, Canada and France—all among countries allied against Nazi Germany and its Axis powers during the war. Their inspirational memories and observations remind us of a time when cooperation and good will among peace-seeking nations arose victorious over evil.

The Introduction by Jeffrey Hahn briefly describes Russian-American cooperation and competition cycles as they are related to the Cold War and *détente* between the former Soviet Union and the United States. The articles of Alexander Dolitsky, Blake Smith and Ivan Negenblya, using both primary and secondary accounts, support Hahn's concept that common interests among the Allies determined their foreign policies and military missions. The article "Women Aviators during World War II and on the Alaska-Siberia Airway," by Miriam Lancaster, justly recognizes the contributions of both the American Women Airforce Service Pilots (WASP) and the Soviet women pilots to the Allied victory. The work of these pilots also set the foundation for women's equal rights in the United States and Russia in the decades following the war.

The presenters' remarks, offered at the Dedication of the WWII Alaska-Siberia Lend-Lease Plaza in Fairbanks in August of 2005, and at the Dedication of the Lend-Lease Memorial in Fairbanks in August 2006, and published here in their entirety, are at once inspiring, factual, emotional, and visionary. In one voice, the presenters acknowledge the significance of the Allies' cooperation against a common enemy during WWII. This historic cooperation serves as a lesson for today's new challenges, and also points out the necessity for peace-seeking nations to cooperate against global terrorism and other regional conflicts that are threatening the world today.

This book is a testimonial source for students of history, political science, ethnohistory, anthropology, and for anyone interested in the history of World War II. The thorough and novel research by the authors, colorful and detailed maps, original and dramatic stories of the participants in the Alaska-Siberia Airway, and authentic photographs of that period of time make this book both educational and entertaining.

Alexander B. Dolitsky
Chairman/Project Manager
Alaska-Siberia Research Center
Juneau, Alaska

Preface II

For many Americans, Russia is an enigmatic, far-off nation. For Alaskans, Russia is our neighbor. We share a common historical bond, international boundary, and natural resources.

Neighbors do not always agree; sometimes there are disputes. But at times they also find a way to live in peace and to cooperate for their common good. This has been the history of the relationship between Russia and Alaska.

Long before the arrival of Europeans, the Natives along the Bering Strait traded, but there were also battles. When the first Russian fur hunters arrived in the 18th century, they nearly exterminated the sea otter population, and enslaved aboriginal people. Later, more enlightened Russian governors and missionaries realized they needed the Natives, just to survive. They created a new class of people—*Creoles*. These were children of Russian fathers and Native mothers. Many of these *Creoles* were educated and went on to fill important offices in the Russian-American Company and in the Russian Orthodox Church.

After the purchase of Alaska by the United States in 1867, there were further disagreements between the Russian and American governments, but there was also cooperation during this period, as in the 1911 Fur Seal Treaty and the start of the reindeer industry in Northwest Alaska in 1891. Later, during the Soviet era, the border between Alaska and Soviet Russia was closed to traffic and trade. The onset of World War II and the implementation of the Lend-Lease program brought cooperation, but, given the historical tensions, disputes persisted—as we see in some of the first-hand accounts published here. Nevertheless, all along the Airway, Alaskans and Soviets set aside their differences in the interest of the program's success.

In the post-war period, relations between the United States and the Soviet Union again cooled. The Cold War period was a time filled with fear and apprehension on both sides. Then, Soviet President Mikhail Gorbachev and the United States President Ronald Reagan reached an agreement that Soviet and Alaskan Natives along the shores of the Bering Strait could once again freely visit each other without government visas. Because of his efforts, the University of Alaska Southeast in 1990 awarded an honorary doctorate to President Gorbachev—the first Russian or Soviet president to receive such an award in America.

Today the relationship between Russia and Alaska is one of cooperation between neighbors. Governmental agencies on both sides are working together to protect our shared natural resources, with Russian and Alaskan scientists coming together annually for environmental discussions. The Beringia International Heritage Park extends across the Bering Strait into Alaska and Siberia, and the Russian Orthodox faith is alive and well in many Alaskan communities.

The Alaska-Siberia Lend-Lease monument in Fairbanks stands as more than a tribute to those who served in World War II. It is symbolic for all peace-seeking nations. For those who see it, there is a greater message; that is, when neighboring regions and nations set aside their differences and help each other, there can be peace, freedom, and security on planet Earth.

Wallace M. Olson
Professor of Anthropology (Emeritus)
University of Alaska Southeast
Juneau, Alaska

Foreword

The Alaska-Siberia (ALSIB) Airway, along which American and Soviet political and military authorities, with additional assistance from Canada, planned and implemented the transport of crucial aircraft to the Soviet Union at a time when that country seemed on the verge of military occupation, remains one of the great untold stories of World War II. On the ALSIB Airway, ordinary but remarkable airmen, soldiers, seamen, and local citizens in the Pacific Northwest, Alaska, and the Soviet Far East, working in an area of harsh climate and uncharted air routes, carried out, at great danger to themselves, the plans of their governments. In this volume, for the first time, the full story of the ALSIB Airway during World War II is told. This work honors in a special way those who lost their lives to keep the supply of Allied equipment to the Soviet Union open.

The creation and sustenance of the ALSIB Airway was by no means easy. Deep mistrust of American and Allied motivations made it difficult to implement the agreement. Stalinist suspicions ruled out plans for the continuing presence of American and Allied troops in the Soviet Far East. In turn, infrastructure to accommodate Soviet military personnel to be stationed in Alaska in a manner separate from American forces took some time to develop. But, beginning in September of 1942, cooperation proceeded rapidly. Collegiality between American, Allied, and Soviet forces grew over time. Even more importantly, the ALSIB Airway, in addition to nearly 8,000 aircraft, was able to deliver vital amounts of military equipment and food supplies to the Soviet Union.

Given the sheer levels of aircraft deliveries alone, one cannot deny the essential role that the ALSIB Airway played in the defeat of Nazi Germany and its Axis powers. One also cannot deny the amazing sacrifices of American, Allied, and Soviet personnel, who risked their lives to create a lifeline of support that saved the lives of many citizens in all of the participating countries.

This book brings the whole story of this cooperation into focus. A highly prestigious group of U.S., Canadian and Russian scholars and policy makers in this volume trace the U.S. and Soviet motivations to form an alliance during the war, the personal stories of the men and women who cooperated in running the ALSIB operation, the 2006 consecration of the memorial to the ALSIB Airway in Fairbanks, and the legacy of American-Soviet cooperation, of which the Airway was a part. For anyone interested in the history and development of Soviet-American and now Russian-American relations, this volume is essential reading.

Robert Huber, Ph.D.
President
National Council for Eurasian and East European Research
Seattle, Washington, U.S.A.

Introduction

Russian-American Relations: Competition and Cooperation

Jeffrey W. Hahn, Ph.D.
Professor of Political Science
Villanova University, Villanova, PA, U.S.A.

The purpose of this introduction is to place the story of cooperation along the Alaska-Siberia Lend-Lease Airway during WWII into a larger context — the development of Russian-American relations over time. Since 1917, relations between Russia and the United States have alternated between periods of competition and cooperation. My thesis is that whether relations have been cooperative or competitive has depended on the degree to which the leaders of the two sides have perceived that they have a common interest. This was clearly the case during WWII when the two countries allied in the face of Hitler's aggression in Europe; the Lend-Lease cooperation was a particularly clear and dramatic example of that. At the time the memorial to Lend-Lease operation was unveiled in Fairbanks, Alaska, on August 27, 2006, the two countries again found themselves cooperating in the face of another common enemy—this time, the threat of global terrorism.

Initial American reaction to Soviet Russia was hostile. In 1917, after the October Revolution in Russia, the U.S. joined other European countries in efforts to weaken the *Bolshevik* regime. They originally supported a *"Cordon Sanitaire"* [1] intended to isolate the *Bolshevik* government diplomatically. In fact, until 1933 the U.S. government refused to recognize the Communist government in Soviet Russia. In the 1930s, however, both countries increasingly found a common interest in their shared opposition to the emergence of fascism in Europe. From 1941 to 1945, they entered into an alliance against Nazi Germany and its Axis powers.

After 1945, relations between the Soviet Union and the United States continued to alternate between cooperation and competition. The period from the end of 1945 to about 1965 was a time of great hostility known as the beginning of the "Cold War" — cold only because actual military conflict did not occur. American policy, based on a perception of the Soviet Union as an expansionist power, was one of "containment." The Soviet Union was seen as an imperialistic power whose communist ideology justified its global ambitions. Soviet expansion could only be deterred by the threat of countervailing power. Containment theory received concrete expression in Europe in the NATO alliance and was later extended to alliances in Asia and the Middle East. By 1965, the Soviet Union was encircled by these hostile alliances.

At the end of the 1960s, the initial phase of the Cold War was replaced by a new period of cooperation known as *"détente."* Again, cooperation grew out of a common interest—this time, a shared desire to control the growth of nuclear weapons. Although the recognition of this common interest can be seen in the 1967 Non-Proliferation Treaty, *détente* reached its zenith with the Strategic

---

[1] French Prime Minister Georges Clemenceau is credited with the first use of the phrase as a metaphor for ideological containment. In March of 1919, he urged the newly independent border states that had broken away from *Bolshevist* Russia to form a defensive union and thus quarantine the spread of communism to Western Europe; he called such an alliance a *cordon sanitaire.* This is still probably the most famous use of the phrase, though it is sometimes used more generally to describe a set of buffer states that form a barrier against a larger, ideologically hostile state. According to historian André Fontaine, Clemenceau's *cordon sanitaire* marked the real beginning of the Cold War; thus, it would have started in 1919 and not in the mid-1940s as most historians contend. [Editor].

Arms Limitation Treaty (SALT) of 1972. The Anti-Ballistic Missile Treaty (ABM Treaty) in particular was evidence that both sides accepted the concept of Mutual Assured Destruction (MAD), which is based on the assumption that the security of both sides depends on the ability of each to destroy the other. The other important result of *détente*, of course, was the political settlement in Europe known as the Helsinki Agreement, signed in 1975, which signaled an acceptance by all parties of a territorial status *quo* in Europe.

By the late nineteen seventies, however, cooperation was replaced once again by competition. First, the Carter administration (1976-1980) made human rights issues a priority in its foreign policy and accused the Soviet Union of violating them, pointing to the issue of Jewish emigration to the West in particular. It was when Ronald Reagan became the U.S. president in 1980, however, that relations became so confrontational that one could speak of a new "Cold War." Going beyond human rights issues, Reagan condemned the communist Soviet Union as an "Evil Empire" and abandoned the SALT process of limiting arms, arguing instead that nuclear arms must be reduced to the levels established in the original Strategic Arms Reduction Treaty (START). Furthermore, Reagan insisted that the Soviet Union had forsaken *détente* by increasing its nuclear and conventional military forces. His response was to deploy a new generation of medium range missiles in Europe and to propose a comprehensive missile defense system known as the Satellite Defense Initiative (SDI) or "Star Wars." By 1985, all negotiations between the Soviet Union and the United States had ended.

Relations between the Soviet Union and the United States entered a new period of cooperation after Mikhail Gorbachev became general secretary of the Communist Party of the Soviet Union in 1985. Gorbachev adopted a new approach to Soviet foreign policy, which he called "New Thinking." For Soviet-American relations, "New Thinking" applied to security meant that under Gorbachev's leadership important agreements on reducing weapons could be achieved. The first breakthrough on this issue came in 1987, when the two countries signed the Intermediate Nuclear Force Agreement (INF) eliminating all medium range missiles in Europe. This was followed by the Conventional Forces in Europe Agreement (CFE) in 1990, a new Strategic Arms Reduction Treaty (START I) in 1991, and other agreements on weapons.

Along with these remarkable achievements in the area of military relations, other issues that had been sources of conflict between Soviet Russia and the United States also began to find resolution. By 1989, the U.S.S.R. had withdrawn from Afghanistan. The Berlin wall came down in the same year and free elections in the communist nations of East Europe brought non-communist governments to power, for the most part without violence. Perhaps the most compelling evidence for the emergence of a new world order in which the Soviet Union would cooperate with the United States to preserve world peace was Soviet support at the United Nations for the use of force against Iraqi aggression in Kuwait. In short, by 1991, all the major issues of contention between the Soviet Union and the United States were ended. It seemed that a new era of cooperation was in place.

By the end of 1991, however, the U.S.S.R. had disintegrated into its fifteen constituent republics, the largest of which was the Russian Federation. What would this mean for Russian-American relations? At first, the cooperative relationship that had developed under *Perestroika* (economic restructuring) and *Glasnost* (freedom of expression and political openness) continued to characterize relations between post-communist Russia and the United States. President Yeltsin and his foreign minister, Andrei Kozyrev, seemed committed to a pro-western orientation. For one thing, they continued to support UN sanctions against Iraq. In the area of nuclear arms reduction, they joined with the U.S. and the former Soviet republics of Ukraine, Belarus, and Kazakhstan to sign a protocol for START I in Lisbon, Portugal in 1992, which would enable START I to be implemented by returning all nuclear weapons in the former Soviet republics to Russia. In January 1993, shortly before he left office, President George Walker Bush signed the START II agreement with President Yeltsin, calling for the reduction of nuclear weapons to half of their previous levels.

By the end of 1994, however, relations began once again to shift. In foreign policy, debate in Russia over whether continued cooperation with the West truly served Russian national interests was growing. Those arguing that American and Russian interests no longer coincided could point to a number of issues: American criticism of Russia's actions in Chechnya in 1995; NATO expansion to the East including Poland, Hungary and the Czech Republic in 1997; the use of NATO military forces against Serbia, first in Bosnia in 1994, and then in Kosovo in 1999; and growing differences over Russian relations with Iraq and Iran. As a result, although the U.S. Senate ratified START II in 1995, by 2000, the Russian Parliament had still refused to do so. Perhaps nothing made Russia more concerned about American intentions than the growing consensus in the U.S. government in support of the ballistic missile defense system, in violation of the 1972 ABM treaty. In short, by the time he left office on December 31, 1999, Yeltsin could accurately describe relations between East and West as a "Cold Peace."

When Vladimir Putin became acting president of Russia on January 1, 2000, little was known about him or his views on foreign policy. The first sense of what direction he might take came even before his inauguration as president in May 2000, when as "acting president" he managed to achieve what Yeltsin could not: *Duma* ratification of START II (although with the condition that the ABM Treaty remain in force). This, coupled with his inaugural speech emphasizing the importance of economic growth and the need to integrate Russia's economy into the global economy, suggested a return to a more pro-western orientation.

From the American side, the year 2000 was dominated by the race for president. Relations with Russia were not an important issue in the campaign. After taking office in January of 2001, the initial attitude of the Bush administration toward Russia was cool. Nevertheless, the administration's general indifference toward Russia had begun to change, even before the events of September 11, 2001. During their first meeting in Slovenia in June 2001, Bush and Putin appeared to establish a warm personal relationship. Said Bush, "I looked the man in the eye. I found him to be very straight forward and trustworthy... I was able to get a sense of his soul."[2] After September 11, 2001, the dynamics of Russian-American relations completely changed to a better prospect. Once again, it is because of the perception of leaders on both sides that they have a common interest—this time in defeating the terrorism associated with radical Islamic fundamentalism.

Despite continuing differences on a number of issues, ranging from the sale of nuclear reactors to Iran and Russian criticism of the Bush administration's decision to invade Iraq, the fact is that today, as in the past, Russian-American relations continue to depend on mutual perceptions of common interests. For now, at least, those common interests compel both sides to cooperate just as they did with the Lend-Lease partnership during World War II. The following chapters provide a diverse and comprehensive overview of this remarkable cooperation—one that will serve as a benchmark for future studies on this important subject.

---

[2] As reported by Frank Bruni, in "Leaders' Words at First Meeting are Striking for Warm Tone," *New York Times*, June 17, 2001.

The Alaska-Siberia Airway: From the Home Front to the Front Lines

The Alaska-Siberia Lend-Lease Program During World War II

Alexander B. Dolitsky
Chairman/Director
Alaska-Siberia Research Center
Juneau, Alaska

> *"The structure of world peace cannot be the work of one man, or one party, or one Nation...It must be a peace which rests on the cooperative effort of the whole world."*
>
> **Franklin Delano Roosevelt, March 1, 1945**
> *Address to Congress on the Yalta Conference*

The aim of this article is twofold. First, we seek to capture some of the oral history of North American and Soviet participants in the Alaska-Siberia Lend-Lease program. Although many Alaskans assisted the Soviets during the war, to date oral history of this period is virtually absent. Such testimony is urgently needed not only to provide an accurate portrayal of Soviet-American relations during World War II, but also to preserve the memories of those who participated in the Alaska-Siberia Lend-Lease program.

The article's second aim is to demonstrate how the domestic needs of the United States, not purely patriotic or ideological motives, once did and might again determine the direction of its foreign policies and external affairs. Not until 16 years after its inception did the United States recognize the U.S.S.R. *de jure* and *de facto*. And when, on November 16, 1933, the United States and the Soviet Union finally did confirm their first diplomatic agreement,[1] hostility between the two countries continued.

---

[1] A. P. Zatsarinsky, *Ekonomicheskiye otnosheniya SSSR s zarubezhnymi stranami, 1917–1967* [Economic Relations of the U.S.S.R. with Foreign Countries, 1917–1967]. Moscow, 1967, [hereinafter Zatsarinsky, *Ekonomicheskiye otnosheniya SSSR*], p. 72.

Yet, despite persistent political tensions, in the summer of 1941 the United States offered the U.S.S.R. a generous Lend-Lease program that expressed its desire for close collaboration against a common enemy: Nazi Germany and its Axis powers. In exploring why the United States would offer such substantial support to its former ideological and political enemy, we find ourselves asking: Must history between nations with different economic and political structures be a static phenomenon, with little or no change in their relations? Or is that history in constant flux based on immediate needs and distribution of forces?

Stalin's Tragic Error and the Nazi Germany Invasion of the Soviet Union

On August 23, 1939, the Soviet Union astounded the world by signing a non-aggression treaty with Nazi Germany. The Hitler-Stalin Pact meant that the Nazi leaders now had a "green light" to attack

Figure 1   *(modified after Catchpole, 1990, p. 30)*

Poland and other democracies without fear of resistance from the Red Army. With the signing of the Nazi-Soviet Pact, the conditions for the start of World War II were set. On September 1, 1939, Nazi Germany attacked Poland, and, on September 17, the Red Army advanced to the eastern part of the country, claiming their share of old Russian Poland. Several days after the German invasion of Poland, Britain and France, honoring their commitments to Poland, promptly declared war on Nazi Germany and the other Axis powers.

Not only did Stalin place an almost naïve faith in the 1939 Non-Aggression Pact, but up until June of 1941, provided Hitler with all sorts of raw materials and logistical support to feed the Nazi war machine. Then, on June 22, 1941, Nazi Germany launched a massive attack against the Soviet Union; the *Operation Barbarossa* had begun. One hundred and fifty-three German divisions crossed the Soviet border along a wide front, while German planes carried out heavy bombing of border points, airfields, railway stations and towns. At the same time, Romania, Hungary, and Finland sent a combined total of 37 divisions against the Soviet Union. Along the Soviet borders, 190 divisions comprising 5.5 million men, 3,712 tanks, 4,950 planes, 47,260 guns and mortars, and 193 military ships amassed.[2] Fascist Italy also declared war on the Soviet Union, and Spain and Bulgaria further aided Germany. At the same time, Japan held a million soldiers of the well-trained *Kwantung* Army ready for action along the Soviet Far Eastern borders.

The situation along the Eastern Front at the beginning of the invasion proved extremely unfavorable for the Soviet Army. The Soviets suffered devastating damage from enemy air attacks that destroyed almost the entire Soviet Air Force in the first week of the invasion—4,017 out of the 7,700 aircraft in the western Soviet Union.[3] By early July of 1941, the Germans occupied Lithuania, a large part of Latvia, and the western territories of Belorussia and the Ukraine. German forces were approaching the Western Dvina River and the upper reaches of the Dnieper River. Through unparalleled acts of bravery on the part of thousands of Soviet soldiers, by mid-July 1941 the enemy was halted near Kiev, and remained stopped for 73 days. The *Wehrmacht* killed or captured more than 660,000 Soviets—about one third of the Red Army—in the battles of Kiev. The battles at Kiev and Uman would prove to be the greatest defeats in the history of the Russian people.[4] As a result of the defeat, the north, center, and south were left wide open to rapid German advance (Figure 1).

By November of 1941, the Germans occupied the Baltic States, Byelorussia, Moldavia, most of the Ukraine, the Crimea, and a large part of Karelia, east of Finland. They had also seized considerable territory around Leningrad and Moscow (Figure 1). Before the war, those occupied parts of the country had contained 40 percent of the total population of the Soviet Union, and had produced 63 percent of the nation's coal, 58 percent of its steel, and 38 percent of its grain. Human losses were enormous, and the Soviet people's independence was at stake once again.[5]

To Help or Not to Help? This is the Question.

To help Western Allies fight the Nazi war machine in Europe, U.S. President Franklin Roosevelt in early 1941 introduced in the Congress the Lend-Lease Bill, titled "An Act Further to Promote the Defense of the United States." The bill was intensely debated throughout the United States, with most strident opposition coming from isolationists and anti-Roosevelt Republicans. Nevertheless, on March 11, 1941, the Congress approved the Lend-Lease Act, granting to the President plenary power to "sell, transfer title to, exchange, lease, lend," or arrange in whatever manner he deemed necessary, the delivery of military materials or military information to the government of a friendly country, if its defense against aggression was vitally important for the defense of the United States. The passing of the Lend-Lease Act was in effect an economic declaration of war against Nazi Germany and its Axis powers. Most Americans were prepared to take that risk rather than to see Britain collapse, leaving the

---

[2] A. M. Soskin, *Istoriya KPSS* [History of the Communist Party of the Soviet Union]. Moscow: Politizdat, 1972, vol. 4, [hereinafter Soskin, *Istoriya KPSS*], p. 34.

[3] Alexander Boyd, *The Soviet Air Force Since 1918*. New York: Stein and Day Publishers, 1977, [hereinafter Boyd, *The Soviet Air Force*], pp. 110-111.

[4] Brian Catchpole, *A Map History of Russia*. London: Butler and Tanner Ltd., 1990, p. 66.

[5] B. D. Datsyuk, *Istoriya SSSR,* vol. 2 [History of the U.S.S.R., vol. 2]. Moscow: Mysl, 1972, p. 277; M. R. Kim, *History of the U.S.S.R.: The Era of Socialism*. Moscow: Progress Publisher, 1982, [hereinafter Kim, *History of the U.S.S.R.*], pp. 358-62.

Franklin D. Roosevelt signing the Lend-Lease Act. After the passage of the Lend-Lease Act on March 11, 1941, Roosevelt soon found himself signing the Declaration of War against Japan, in December 1941.

U.S. to face the Nazi Axis alone.

After the Nazi German invasion of the Soviet Union, the governments of Britain and the United States declared their support for the U.S.S.R. in its struggle against fascist aggression. On June 23, 1941, President Franklin D. Roosevelt made the statement to the media that "Hitler's armies are today the chief dangers to the Americas." This statement contained no clear promise of aid to the Soviets but stated clearly the State Department's policy. The next day, on June 24, 1941, Roosevelt announced at a press conference that the United States would give all possible help to the Soviet people in their struggle against Nazi Germany and its Axis powers. That same day, President Roosevelt released Soviet assets in American banks, which had been frozen after the Soviet attack on Finland on November 30, 1939; this enabled the Soviets immediately to purchase 59 fighters. Preliminary discussions between U.S., British, and Soviet officials on deliveries of arms and other vital supplies began on June 26, 1941.[6] A British credit line was subsequently opened on August 16, 1941, and arms deliveries from England immediately initiated, with the American Lend-Lease principles as guidelines. Soon after the U.S.-Soviet Lend-Lease agreement was signed, on June 11, 1942, the British Lend-Lease agreement to the Soviet Union was formalized in a British-Soviet agreement signed on June 26th.

Many conservatives in the United States argued vociferously against the U.S.-Soviet pact, asserting that America's aid should be disbursed only to proven friends, such as Great Britain and China. In congressional debates on the subject in late July and August, isolationists insisted that to aid the Soviet Union was to aid communism. In June of 1941, Senator (later President) Harry Truman expressed common American sentiments on Hitler's invasion of the Soviet Union: "If we see that Germany is winning, we ought to help Russia, and if we see Russia is winning, we ought to help Germany, and that way let them kill as many as possible."[7]

At the same time, others thought the Russian front might be America's salvation. In July of 1941, a public opinion poll indicated that 54 percent of Americans opposed Soviet aid, but by September those opposed registered only 44 percent, and those who favored helping the Soviet Union had risen to 49 percent.[8] Roosevelt's approach to aiding the Soviets was cautious but intuitively optimistic. He distrusted them but did not think that they, in contrast to the Germans, intended to conquer Europe. He viewed Hitler's armies as the chief threat to the Americas. Roosevelt calculated the Soviets would

---

[6] Robert H. Jones, *The Roads to Russia*. Norman, Okla., 1969, [hereinafter Jones, *The Roads to Russia*], p. 35.

[7] David M. Kennedy, Lizabeth Cohen, Thomas A. Bailey, *The American Pageant*. New York: Houghton Mifflin Company, 2002, p. 822.

[8] Jones, *The Roads to Russia*, p. 55.

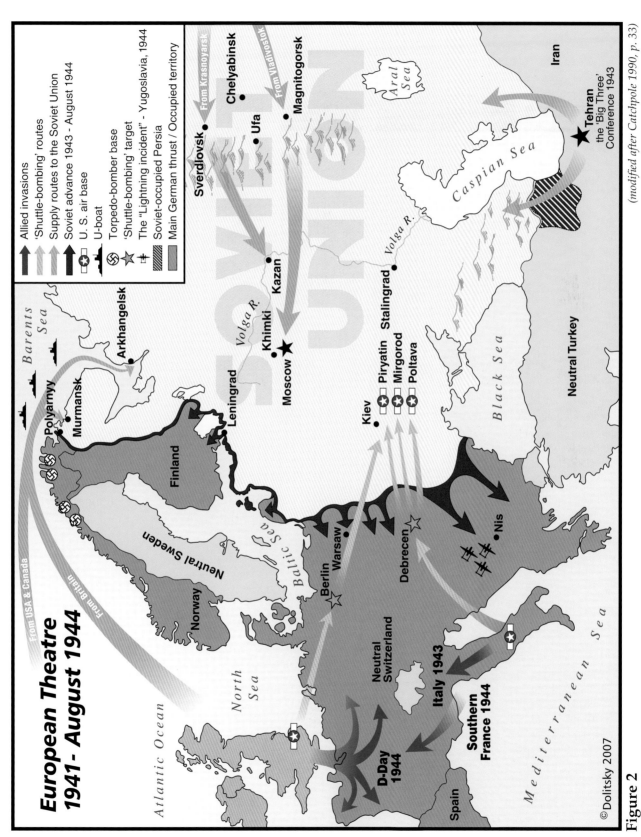

European Theatre 1941- August 1944

© Dolitsky 2007

Legend:
- Allied invasions
- 'Shuttle-bombing' routes
- Supply routes to the Soviet Union
- Soviet advance 1943 - August 1944
- U. S. air base
- U-boat
- Torpedo-bomber base
- 'Shuttle-bombing' target
- The "Lightning incident" – Yugoslavia, 1944
- Soviet-occupied Persia
- Main German thrust / Occupied territory

Atlantic Ocean

Barents Sea

North Sea

Baltic Sea

Black Sea

Mediterranean Sea

Caspian Sea

Aral Sea

SOVIET UNION

From USA & Canada
From Britain
From Krasnoyarsk
From Vladivostok

Polyarnyy
Murmansk
Arkhangelsk
Norway
Neutral Sweden
Finland
Leningrad
Moscow
Khimki
Kazan
Sverdlovsk
Ufa
Chelyabinsk
Magnitogorsk
Volga R.
Stalingrad
Kiev
Piryatin
Mirgorod
Poltava
Berlin
Warsaw
Debrecen
Nis
Neutral Switzerland
Spain
Italy 1943
Southern France 1944
D-Day 1944
Neutral Turkey
Iran
Tehran the 'Big Three' Conference 1943

(modified after Catchpole 1990, p. 33)

Figure 2

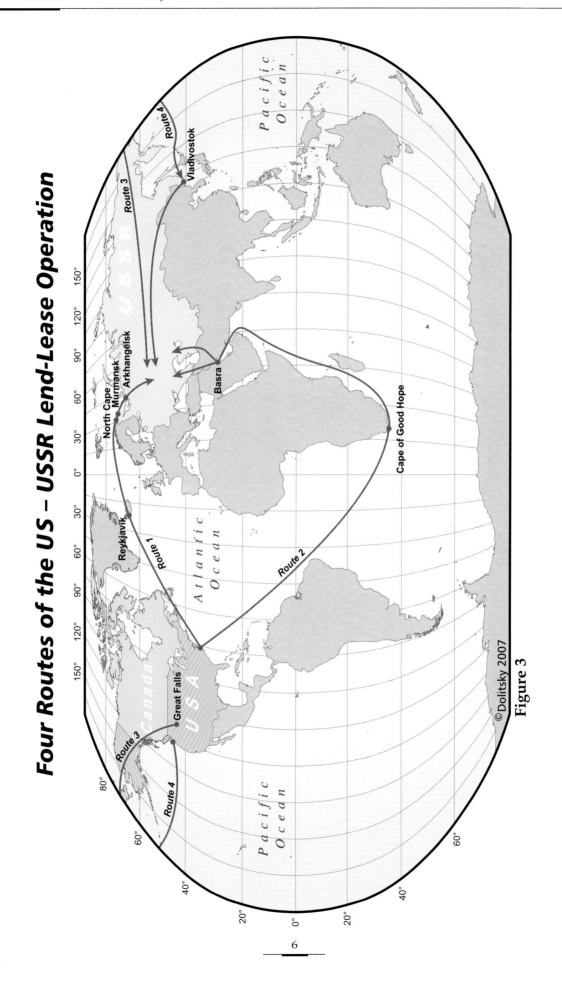

Four Routes of the US – USSR Lend-Lease Operation

©Dolitsky 2007

Figure 3

resist the German assault longer than anyone anticipated, which would help the British and perhaps preclude America's involvement.[9] The president relied heavily on the assessment of senior advisers Harry Hopkins and Averell Harriman, who urged him to bring the Soviet Union under a Lend-Lease agreement. But Roosevelt still held back.

In July of 1941, Roosevelt appointed Harry Hopkins, Constantine Oumansky, and Arthur Purvis to an intergovernmental committee on Soviet aid, and granted Hopkins' request to go to the Soviet Union. Meeting with Stalin and other Soviet authorities, Hopkins came to the conclusion that the Soviets would withstand the German attack, and cabled Washington his opinion to that effect. In early September of 1941, Roosevelt decided to send Averell Harriman, a large investor in the Soviet Union since 1918, to Moscow as a special adviser on Lend-Lease matters. Harriman was charged, along with British representatives, with working out a temporary aid program.

US-Soviet Lend-Lease Negotiations

From September 29 to October 1, 1941, representatives from Britain, the Soviet Union and the United States attended a conference held in Moscow. There, a plan was drawn up for delivery of armaments, equipment, and foodstuffs to the Soviet Union. The U.S.S.R. in turn agreed to provide strategic raw materials to Britain and the United States.[10] During the conference, Harriman for the first time suggested delivery of United States aircraft to the Soviet Union via Alaska and Siberia using American crews. But Stalin rejected this idea unconditionally, perhaps to avoid provoking Japan. Despite some political tension at the Moscow conference, on October 30 Roosevelt approved, and on November 4, 1941 Stalin accepted, $1 billion in aid, to be repaid in ten years, interest free.[11]

Although the Soviet government was pleased with the aid package, they still complained that the Allies had taken no serious military action against Germany, and the Soviet Union continued to bear alone the brunt of the war. The Soviets suggested that Britain and the U.S. open a second front in France or the Balkans, or send troops through Iran (which the Soviets and British had jointly occupied in August), in order to preclude Germany from attacking the Ukraine from the south. The Soviet government continued to insist that opening a second front in Europe would relieve pressure from enemy attacks on the Eastern Front. The Allies, however, were reluctant to initiate this plan at the time because of lack of forces for a second front, due to Allied involvement in the Pacific and North African theaters. Churchill, Stalin, and Roosevelt, in tacit acknowledgment of the fact that they had not yet reached agreement on joint war or peace aims, thus limited their 1941 pact to Lend-Lease support to the Soviet Union.[12]

On July 7, 1941, a Soviet delegation flew from Vladivostok to Nome, and then on to Kodiak and Seattle, for secret talks with American officials regarding aircraft deliveries to the U.S.S.R. and the feasibility of Pacific supplies routes. The Soviet and American delegations discussed several possible routes for shipping planes and war materials to the U.S.S.R. The first was a sea route across the North Atlantic and around the North Cape to the ice-free Arctic ports of Murmansk and Archangelsk (Figures 2, 3). This route was shorter but by far the more dangerous of those considered because of regular patrols in the area by the German navy and the Axis powers. Another discussed route would transport the materials by ship across the Atlantic Ocean, around South Africa's Cape of Good Hope, and then north to the Iraqi port of Basra, where supplies would be loaded onto trains and trucks and transported to Soviet Central Asia and Azerbaijan via Iran (Figures 2, 3). This route, too, had serious

---

[9] Arnold A. Offner, *The Origins of the Second World War*. Malabar, Fla., 1986, [hereinafter Offner, *Origins*], p. 206.

[10] Kim, *History of the U.S.S.R.*, p. 368.

[11] Offner, *Origins*, p. 207; Eduard A. Ivanyan, *Encyclopedia of Russian-American Relations (XVIII-XX Centuries)*. Moscow: International Relations, 2001, Appendix.

[12] P. N. Pospelov, *Istoriya Kommunistecheskoy Partii (1938-1945)* [History of the Communist Party of the Soviet Union: 1938-1945], vol. 5, part 1. Moscow, 1970, p. 543; Offner, *Origins*, p. 208.

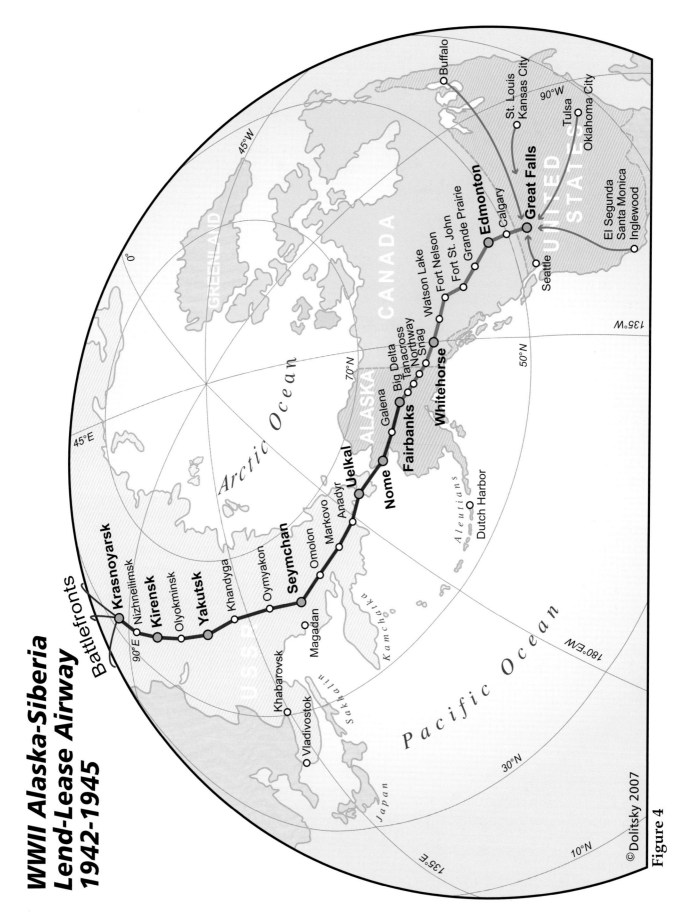

**WWII Alaska-Siberia
Lend-Lease Airway
1942-1945**

©Dolitsky 2007

Figure 4

drawbacks—not only would the goods take too long to reach the U.S.S.R., the desert sands in Iran were notorious for infiltrating and ruining aircraft engines.[13]

On October 1, 1941, the United States and the U.S.S.R. signed the First Soviet Lend-Lease Protocol to provide aid to the Soviet Union. The U.S.S.R. accepted most of the Lend-Lease terms, but specific details had yet to be worked out. On May 29, 1942, Vyacheslav Molotov, a Soviet Foreign Commissar and the right hand of Joseph Stalin on foreign affairs, arrived in the United States to discuss Lend-Lease matters. It was the Soviet dignitary's first official visit on American soil. Being cautious and uncertain in this formerly hostile country, he carried in his luggage some sausages, a piece of black bread, and a pistol to defend his person if the need arose.[14] During Molotov's visit, President Roosevelt raised two possibilities: (1) that American aircraft be flown to the U.S.S.R. via Alaska and Siberia, and (2) that Soviet ships pick up Lend-Lease supplies from America's west coast ports for ferrying across the Pacific to Vladivostok and other Soviet Far Eastern ports—in addition to two other routes (the northern run to Murmansk and the Iran route) proposed earlier in July 1941. Roosevelt noted that by using the Alaska-Siberia route, which would connect to the Trans-Siberian Railway, Lend-Lease supplies could more quickly and safely reach the Ural industrial complex around Magnitogorsk (Figures 2, 3, 4).

After careful consideration of various proposals, the best route for planes seemed to be via Alaska and Siberia. Although great distances were involved and the worst possible weather conditions would be encountered, the planes would be delivered in flying condition and the possibility of enemy interference was remote. American support for the Alaska-Siberia route was also based on the hope that eventually Siberian air bases would be used for bombing raids on Japan.[15] The Soviets, however, were hesitant to use this route, believing the Alaska-Siberia route to be too dangerous and impractical. It was also thought that Siberian cities would not be able to accommodate the busy air traffic, and that the presence of Americans in the Soviet Far East would be unwanted. The Soviets were also afraid that the Pacific supply routes, and the Alaska-Siberia route in particular, might provoke Japanese military actions against the Soviet Union. Nevertheless, faced with losses mounting on the sea run to Murmansk, and given the great distances involved in the Middle East route, the Soviets finally agreed to open the Alaska-Siberia air route on Aug. 3, 1942.[16] The final Lend-Lease agreement, signed in Washington, D.C. on June 11, 1942, was titled "Mutual Aid Agreement Between the United States of America and the Union of Soviet Socialist Republics."[17]

The Alaska-Siberia delivery route finally became a reality in August of 1942. A North American air transport route connecting Great Falls in Montana, Edmonton and Whitehorse in Canada, and Fairbanks, Galena, and Nome in Alaska was established (Figure 4). A major airfield constructed in Nome served as the jumping off point for planes headed for Siberia. Once inside Siberia, airplanes continued on their long trip from Uelkal through Markovo, Seymchan, Yakutsk, Kirensk, and finally to Krasnoyarsk. In Krasnoyarsk, fresh pilots took over, flying the newly-arrived aircraft westward via Omsk, Sverdlovsk, and Kazan to the Russian battlefronts (Figure 4). Over the program's three years of operations, nearly 8,000 aircraft would be sent through Great Falls, Montana and Ladd Field, Alaska for transfer to the Soviet Union.

The Russians are Coming

On August 26, 1942, the first Soviet envoys, Col. Piskunov and Alexis A. Anisimov, members of the Soviet Purchasing Commission, arrived in Nome. On September 3, 1942, the first Soviet aircraft arrived

---

[13]   Stan Cohen, *The Forgotten War: A Pictoral History of World War II in Alaska and Northwestern Canada*. Missoula, Mont., 1981, vol. 1, [hereinafter Cohen, *Forgotten War*, vol. 1], p. 44.

[14]   James MacGregor Burns, *Roosevelt, the Soldier of Freedom (1940-1945)*. New York, 1970, p. 232; Robert Francaviglia, *The Alaska-Siberia Aircraft Ferry Project (1942-1945)*, [unpublished manuscript, 1973]. Alaska State Library, Juneau, p.1.

[15]   Hubert van Tuyll, *Feeding the Bear: American Aid to the Soviet Union, 1941-1945*. New York, 1989, [hereinafter van Tuyll, *Feeding the Bear*], p. 27.

[16]   Cohen, *Forgotten War*, vol. 1, p. 44.

[17]   Zatsarinsky, *Ekonimicheskiye otnosheniya SSSR*, p. 93.

Soviet military mission arrives in Nome, Alaska on September 3, 1942. The soldiers in helmets and the officer in riding breeches are Americans; the rest are Soviets. Courtesy of USAF.

in Alaska, bringing more mission members to set up a permanent command station at Ladd Field in Fairbanks, and in Nome. By the summer of 1943, many Soviets had been stationed at Fairbanks, Nome, and Galena; at the height of the program anywhere from 150 to 600 Soviet pilots and other personnel resided at Ladd Field alone.[18] Bill Schoeppe, an airplane mechanic and a Technical Representative for North American Aviation, was stationed at Ladd Field in Fairbanks, and then in Nome, from 1942 to 1944. According to his recollection, Soviet service men were stationed only in Alaska.

> *No big thing, but it should be known there were no Russian service men stationed at any of our bases in Great Falls, Edmonton, Whitehorse and Yukon. While on assignment with North American Aviation, I traveled many times to our air bases in Canada and Alaska and never met or never heard of Russian personnel along the ferry route.[19]*

Soviets assigned to work on American soil were ideologically drilled to maintain loyalty to their motherland. Separate facilities were built in Fairbanks and Nome for Soviet officers and other staff, and the Soviet government preferred to use its own interpreters and office personnel—predominantly women in uniform who had passed classified clearance procedures in the Soviet Union before coming to the United States.[20] "I never saw any female Russian transport pilots [in Alaska]," wrote Bill Schoeppe, "and I flew many hours in Russian B-25s from Fairbanks to Nome."[21] In fact, at the time, women pilots in the U.S.S.R. were allowed to fly in combat. Many distinguished themselves and earned their country's highest medal of honor.

---

[18] Cohen, *Forgotten War*, vol. 1, p. 45.

[19] Bill Schoeppe, hand-written correspondence, dated 01/27/93, Dolitsky's private collection.

[20] Bill Schoeppe and Randy Acord, personal communication and written correspondence, 1993, 1995.

[21] Bill Schoeppe, hand-written correspondence, dated 01/27/93, Dolitsky's private collection.

Although the Soviet airmen who were sent to Alaska to pick up the Lend-Lease aircraft were guests in Alaska, and in the Soviet Union the Alaskan mission was regarded as a "rest from combat," they tended to remain aloof from the Americans. On those occasions when Soviets would socialize with Americans, they sometimes expressed their ideological views, but reluctantly and with great caution. For the most part, the Soviets and Americans were cordial toward one another. Some became close acquaintances during and after the war, leaving a lasting mark of good memories of and affection for one another.[22] As Bill Schoeppe wrote,

Bill Schoeppe, an employee of Star Aviation, Inc., in Anchorage in 1940, prior to his deployment to Ladd Field, Fairbanks in 1942. Alexander Dolitsky's collection.

[W]henever there was a gang of pilots in town waiting for airplanes, they roamed the streets of Fairbanks, some buying women's silk stockings and underwear. Most unusual was their use of perfume! Some rough-bearded guys in britches and fine leather boots, [wearing] heavy perfume while partying, which we did every now and again. All men, only lots of drinks and smoking, and all these guys loaded with perfume! Some said it was because they had no anti-perspirant! We'll never forget that high consumption of liquor. All Alaskans and U.S. military personnel drank excessive quantities of alcohol, but the Red Army men beat us by far. Without fail, the Russians laid on the greatest variety and quantity. Each party table in mess halls, most seating 4 to 6 men, contained lots [of] spiced food and at least 5 to 6 quarts of liquor.

The Russian hosts always kept the liquor flowing, so the big restaurant-size glasses were seldom empty. "Down the Hatch" was the constant order as toasts were proposed to Stalin and Roosevelt! These parties usually ended in 2 to 3 hours. We were always amazed how the Russians could put away so much more liquor than Americans.

Bill Schoeppe in December of 1993, in Juneau, Alaska. Alexander Dolitsky's collection.

A few times we were entertained by some fine male dancing: wild whirling and jumping [, the] Gypsy dances were outstanding. Remember especially the pace the musician kept – until they had to step out because they were exhausted![23]

Schoeppe also recalled his occasional meetings with the Soviet Captain Michael Gubin, an engineer of the Nome Permanent Garrison, when both were stationed in Nome. Evidently, Bill Schoeppe did not know at that time that Captain Michael Gubin was a Soviet intelligence officer.[24]

Captain Gubin: engineer-officer in Nome, very friendly, nice fellow; he and his wife and two children lived off base in a small house near the city's center. I lived in a hotel with 3 other factory representatives, and I spent several nice Sundays in the Gubin's home for dinner and drinks. Remember one Sunday so well, friendly conversation with many husky drinks; he

---

[22] Bill Schoeppe, Randy Acord, and Charles Binkley, personal communication, 1993, 1995 and 1998.

[23] Bill Schoeppe, hand-written correspondence, dated 01/27/93, Dolitsky's private collection.

[24] Otis Hays, Jr. *The Alaska-Siberia Connection: The World War II Air Route.* College Station: Texas A&M University Press, 1996, [hereinafter Hays, *The Alaska-Siberia Connection*], p. 171.

spoke good English and we spent many hours talking politics and comparing our form of governments. Stalin, of course, was a big hero, always a toast for Stalin and Roosevelt!

The Captain's wife didn't speak much English but she kept apologizing for the poor furnishings, dishes and silver.

One Sunday, I remember so well, following several drinks we came to the table and large bowls of soup were served, and I assumed that was it! But then the main course was served – a huge beef tongue and vegetables, and dark bread! This is a rich meat, and everyone had to be served seconds. I did not think I would be able to stand up!

I've often thought how rough those times were for Captain's wife – unable to speak English, with two young kids in a small house, no running water and no sewer system, [going from] house to house with horse drawn sled in the winter.[25]

Despite occasional friendly meetings between Soviet and American personnel, Soviet insistence that the planes be in perfect condition before being flown to Siberia caused constant delays and some antagonism between the two commands. According to Bill Schoeppe there were many FBI people in Fairbanks and on the base. He noticed the appearance of many FBI agents, particularly when Soviet top brass were visiting. Schoeppe recalled ongoing Soviet suspicions:

So many things happened in those times and sabotage was blamed too often. For example, the P-39 and P-63 pursuit planes were powered with V-12 liquid cooled Allison engines; so much trouble was encountered, especially during extremely cold weather. These engines had to be warmed at a very high idle; if not, the spark plugs would foul badly. When the temperature is minus 40 to 50°. . . there are

Soviet and American pilots at Nome, Alaska, in 1942. Courtesy of University of Alaska Anchorage.

[25] Bill Schoeppe, hand-written correspondence, dated 12/17/93, Dolitsky's private collection.

Soviet graduates of the Combat Pilots School, in Ulan Ude, USSR, 1943, in cold weather gear. Vasiliy Koshonkin (second from right) took part in ferrying Airacobra P-39s and Kingcobra P-63s from Uelkal to Krasnoyarsk. Courtesy of Anchorage Fine Arts Museum.

many problems. Each engine has 24 spark plugs. 24 x 30 = 720 plugs to be changed, [and it] causes lots of trouble. Usually these plugs would be sand blasted and checked, but for a time the Russians [thought] they were sabotaged and demanded all replacement plugs be factory new . . .

I recall one case that was comical to say the least. P-39 had been grounded in Edmonton; the V-12 engine was mounted behind [the] pilot, [and] a big carburetor mounted on top – between banks and cylinders. One of the mechanics placed a silk cloth over the carburetor to prevent parts falling into the engine. When repairs were complete someone put the cowl-cover over the engine and forgot to remove [the] silk-cover. When the pilot reported low power on arrival to Fairbanks he said, "sabotage again!!"[26]

There were many crashes by both the Soviet and American pilots, caused mainly by weather conditions, but also by poor maintenance, overloading the aircraft, lack of fuel, and, incidentally, a large consumption of hard liquor by Soviet pilots the day before a long and dangerous journey. As Bill Schoeppe recalled, the winter of 1942-43 was extremely cold in Alaska and planes before they could be flown out had to be winterized — in very difficult working conditions — in order to prevent mechanical failure.

---

[26] Ibid.

We had no idea of the number of aircraft that were lost along the ferry route from Edmonton to Whitehorse and Fairbanks due to heavy smoke from forest and muskeg fires, which went wild during the war. Zero visibility was common day after day. Our radio aids to navigation were very poor or nonexistent; this, with low-time, inexperienced pilots, made a tough combination. It was found that many airplanes had ended up 180° off course and out of fuel, so a system of flying in ever-widening circles by rescue planes was initiated, and is still used today in wilderness areas.[27]

From September 1942 to September 1945, 133 planes were lost in North America, and 44 planes in Siberia along the Alaska-Siberia Airway due to severe weather conditions, mechanical problems and pilot error — a total of 2.22 percent of the 7,983 planes that were to be delivered to the Soviets from Great Falls.[28]

Randy Acord, test pilot for the Army Air Forces, Cold Weather Testing Detachment, Ladd Field, Fairbanks, 1944. Alexander Dolitsky's collection via Randy Acord.

Trust but Verify

In four years of war, the United States supplied 14,798 combat aircraft to the Soviet Union. More than half (7,925) of the planes were flown over the Northwest Route through Alaska and accepted at Ladd Field in Fairbanks.[29] Looking back, some American military experts questioned whether the Soviets needed all these aircraft. By the end of 1943, the U.S.S.R. was building a great number of planes in factories in the Ural Mountains and already had technical military superiority over its enemies.[30] In 1943, Soviet industry produced 35,000 airplanes and 24,000 tanks and self-propelled guns, compared with 25,000 airplanes and 18,000 tanks produced by Germany.[31] In fact, despite their smaller industrial capacity and a reduced base of strategic materials, the Soviet Union still produced more military equipment than Germany overall, with a total output during the war of 137,000 aircraft (including 112,100 combat planes), 104,000 tanks and self-propelled guns, and 488,000 artillery pieces.[32]

According to Randy Acord, test pilot for the Army Air Forces at Ladd Field, the Soviet Union was stockpiling Lend-Lease equipment for postwar use, and probably used the air route for espionage.[33] American soldiers of the Korean War (1950-53) were puzzled to see so much American equipment (e.g. jeeps, trucks) captured by American

[27] Bill Schoeppe, hand-written correspondence, dated 01/27/93, Dolitsky's private collection.

[28] Cohen, *Forgotten War*, vol. 1, p. 46; Oleg Chechin, "Rescue of a Soviet Navigator," *Soviet Life*, no. 11, 1989, pp. 39-42; E. E. Jr. Furler, "Beneath the Midnight Sun," *Air Classics*, vol. 20-3, 1984, pp. 25-34; Ivan Negenblya, *Alyaska-Sibir: Trassa Muzhestva* [Alaska-Siberia: the Road of Courage]. Yakutsk, 2000, [hereinafter Negenblya, *Alyaska-Sibir: Trassa Muzhestva*], p. 100, 168.

[29] Jones, *The Roads to Russia*, Table 2, p. 272 (this does not include PBN and PBY patrol planes); Hays, *The Alaska-Siberia Connection*, p. 167.

[30] George Racey Jordan, *From Major Jordan's Diaries*. New York, 1952, [hereinafter Jordan, *Diaries*], pp. 126-27.

[31] Soskin, *Istoriya KPSS*, p. 50.

[32] Kim, *History of the U.S.S.R.*, p. 397.

[33] Randy Acord, personal communication, 1993, 2006.

Officers of the Cold Weather Testing Detachment, Ladd Field, Fairbanks, 1944. Alexander Dolitsky's collection via Randy Acord.

troops during the Korean War.[34] Evidently, the Chinese and Soviets provided military aid to Korea using the very same supplies they had received from the United States several years earlier. American analysts have yet to grasp the full extent and intention of Soviet secrecy during WWII on matters ranging from combat operations to agricultural production. Information would often have to come directly from Stalin, which led some officials to conclude he "apparently was the only individual in the Soviet Union who had the authority to give some information."[35] Some American military experts have alleged that uranium was shipped through Great Falls, and it was also suspected that in May of 1944 U.S. Treasury banknote plates had gone up the air route.[36] Of course, opposing views deny any such Soviet conspiracy in using the route.[37]

---

[34] Gerald Dorsher, a veteran of the Korean War, personal communication 1993, 2006.

[35] Van Tuyll, *Feeding the Bear*, p. 13.

[36] Jordan, *Diaries*, p. 217.

[37] Bill Schoeppe, personal communication, correspondence, and audiotapes, 1993, 1995, Dolitsky's collection.

Much information attesting to the helpful U.S. attitude toward the U.S.S.R. and vice versa during the war remains unknown to the general American public. Assertions by post-war commentators that a thorough evaluation of the Soviet Lend-Lease program might uncover some embarrassing facts likely are due more to the context of the Cold War, and to "global" foreign affair policies that began during the Truman presidency, than to any widespread wrongdoing during the war. This was clear in a House of Representatives hearing on Lend-Lease matters, held during the McCarthy era of the early 1950s, which was tainted with exaggerations and fabrications by members seeking to persecute liberal historians, radical socialists, and anyone perceived as sympathetic to the Soviet Union.[38]

Feeding the Russian Bear

From 1941 to 1945, about $11 billion in war materials and other supplies were shipped to the Soviet Union from the United States over four major routes. In addition to military equipment, the U.S.S.R. received such non-military items as cigarette cases, records, women's compacts, fishing tackle, dolls, playground equipment, cosmetics, food, and even 13,328 sets of false teeth. Soviet requests for food emphasized canned meat (*tushonka*), fats, dried peas and beans, potato chips, powdered soups and eggs, dehydrated fruits and vegetables, and other packaged food items.[39] Although dehydration solved shipping problems to the Soviet Union, such requests also resulted in the rapid expansion of American dehydrating facilities, which eventually influenced the domestic market and the diet of the American people in the post-War period up to the present.[40]

Lend-Lease accounts show that in 1945 alone about 5,100,000 tons of foodstuffs left for the Soviet Union from the United States, at a time that the Soviets' own 1945 total agricultural output reached approximately 53,500,000 tons.[41] If the twelve million individual members of the Soviet Army received all of the foodstuffs that arrived in the U.S.S.R. through Lend-Lease deliveries from the United States, each man and woman would have been supplied with more than half a pound of concentrated food per day for the duration of the war. Undoubtedly, Lend-Lease food proved vital to the maintenance of adequate nutrition levels for Soviets and other Lend-Lease beneficiaries. For example, in 1944, two percent of the United States' food supply was exported to the Soviet Union, 4 percent to other Lend-Lease recipients, 1 percent to commercial exports, and 13 percent to the United States military. This aid was only possible due to sacrifices made by the American people and the enormous increase in American agricultural and industrial production—up 280 percent by 1944 over the 1935-1939 average.[42]

Although the Soviet government tried to minimize the importance of Lend-Lease support by arguing that U.S. supplies to the U.S.S.R. represented only four to ten percent of the total Soviet Union production during the war, the aid items were in fact essential for the nation's survival. For example, while Soviet production of steel was about 9,000,000 tons in 1942, under Lend-Lease, the Soviet Union received about 30 percent, or 3,000,000 tons of steel. The Soviet T-34 tank engine and Soviet aircraft used Lend-Lease aluminum. Copper shipments (about 4,000,000 tons) equaled three-quarters of the entire Soviet copper production for the years 1941-1944. About 800,000 tons of non-ferrous metals (e.g. magnesium, nickel, zinc, lead, tin), 1,000,000 miles of field telegraph wire, 2,120 miles of marine cable and 1,140 miles of submarine cable formed an impressive figure, especially when compared to Soviet production.[43]

The Soviet Union also received essential military items under the Lend-Lease agreement: 14,798 aircraft (not including PBN and PBY patrol planes) from the United States, and nearly 4,570 warplanes from Great Britain—equivalent to 17 percent of the 112,100 warplanes produced in Soviet plants; 9,000

[38] Jay H. Moor, *World War II in Alaska: The Northwest Route. A Bibliography and Guide to Primary Sources*, Alaska Historical Commission Studies in History, no. 175. Anchorage, AK: Alaska Historical Commission, 1985, p. 4.

[39] van Tuyll, *Feeding the Bear*, pp. 152-80.

[40] Alexander Dolitsky, "The Alaska-Siberia Lend-Lease Program," *Alaska at War, 1941-1945*, ed. Fern Chandonnet. Anchorage, Alaska, 1995, p. 337.

[41] Jones, *The Roads to Russia*, p. 218.

[42] Ibid., p. 268.

[43] Ibid., pp. 215-39, Tables I and II, pp. 270-278; van Tuyll, *Feeding the Bear*, pp. 94-103, 114-21, 152-82.

Among His Honors, the Soviet Ace of Aces, an Airacobra pilot, Wears the Distinguished Service Medal Awarded by President Roosevelt.

(Editor's note: The following article is reprinted through the courtesy of Time Magazine).

TIME "ACHTUNG POKRYSHKIN"

Lieutenant-Colonel Alexander Pokryshkin. Airacobra Ace

Sovfoto

Moscow's hero worshippers recently heard the latest: Major (now Lieutenant-Colonel) Alexander Pokryshkin had shot down his 59th enemy plane, was still beyond challenge, the ace of all Allied aces.

Muscovites guessed the tight-knit, blond, blue-eyed ex-mechanic scored his latest triumph over Rumania, where in 1941 he began his fighting career. He was then 28 and middle-aged by U. S. or British fighter-pilot standards. Since then he has fought more than 500 air battles, has been shot down thrice.

Today Pokryshkin commands a regiment — rough equivalent of a U. S. group — in Russia's most famous fighter unit (its other aces: Richkalov, 46; Glinka, 38; Lugansky, 32; Alelyukhin, 29.)

The BELLRINGER, *November, 1943, carried pictures of the Brothers Glinka—Airacobra Aces both—being decorated as Heroes of the*

Soviet Union for the outstanding combat records they had made as P-39 pilots.

Pokryshkin, eloquent only when he talks flying, drinks little, eats and sleeps much. Superstitious, he will not be photographed before a flight. Six months ago he married a Red WAC at the front. On furloughs Pokryshkin goes to Moscow for a round of theaters and tourist sights (he has been seen gawking at the Moscow subway's new, resplendent stations). After the war he wants to be a plane designer.

Brother's Advice. Pokryshkin's mother still lives in Novosibirsk, with the youngest of her four sons. She is a plain old peasant woman, proud of her sons. Recently she wrote to Alexander: "Your brother (also an airman) wants to shift to your unit." Replied Alexander: "Let him prove his mettle." Steady-nerved and self-confident, Pokryshkin is as fatalistic as most combat pilots. In

combat he is cautious and calculating, likes to feel out his enemy before the kill. In the Army's *Red Star* recently he analyzed some airmen's failures: "They have not absorbed . . . the feel of a fighter . . . They are not sly or calculating enough, and they act in a stereotyped manner . . . It is clear that such airmen cannot fight successfully."

Pokryshkin has earned a chestful of medals (including the U. S. Distinguished Service Cross), a bust in his native Novosibirsk. But the highest prize comes through his earphones when he slashes into enemy formations. Then the german flight leaders identify his plane with its cluster of red stars— one for each aircraft downed—and shout.

"*Achtung, Achtung*—Pokryshkin."

It was last fall, right after a battle in which he and nine other Russian Airacobra pilots routed 30 nazi bombers and eight fighter planes, that Pokryshkin learned, through a Soviet newspaper, that he had been awarded the Distinguished Service Medal by President Roosevelt.

"The major earned the medal by his courage and ability to engage the enemy in his American Airacobra fighter plane," the newspaper said. "Pokryshkin has a record of 41 german machines brought down to date. Many of these german buzzards were des-

troyed while he was flying the faithful Airacobra."

Lieutenant-Colonel Pokryshkin has flown a good many combat missions since that day. His score has increased from 41 to 59 nazi planes. But the story of the battle he had just gone through is worth repeating.

Four of the 'Cobras took on the fighters. The other six headed into the nazi bombers' formation. Three of the stukas went down in flames in rapid succession. The rest released their bomb loads on their own forces and

turned back.

The 'Cobras led by Pokryshkin continued their patrol and sighted another group of bombers and fighters and roared into the attack. Three more enemy aircraft were destroyed in this affray and the german bombing party turned tail for home, completely disrupted.

It has been countless missions like this which have made this Russian Airacobra Ace the outstanding fighter pilot of the United Nations.

Page Three

From the June 1944 issue of **Bellringer** *magazine, a publication of the Bell Aircraft Company in Buffalo, NY. Courtesy of the Niagara Aerospace Museum collection, Niagara Falls, NY.*

and to use Soviet resistance for their own mobilization.

Soviet efforts to minimize the role of the Lend-Lease program may have been motivated by considerations of national prestige and image. Only recently have Russian scholars begun to note the significant contributions of Lend-Lease supplies to the war effort. Although during the war the Soviet government gave decorations to a number of Westerners, and it recently honored seamen who had served on the Murmansk run, they still emphasize the small size of Lend-Lease aid in relation to Soviet production and the heroism of the Soviet people in delivering Lend-Lease supplies.[53] To understand the complexity of the Soviet attitude toward Lend-Lease operation, one must treat the subject in the context of Russian and Soviet history, politics, law, traditions and behavioral psychology.

Negotiations for the Repayment of the Lend-Lease Supply

Lend-Lease was a system of transfer to participating countries of military and other materials necessary for conducting the war. Countries receiving aid through Lend-Lease signed a bilateral agreement with the U.S. stipulating that materials destroyed, lost, or used during the war would not be subject to any repayment whatsoever after the end of the war, that materials left over after the war suitable to the needs of the population would be subject to repayment in full or in part by means of long-term credit, that military materials left after the war could be obtained on demand by the U.S. government (although the U.S. government repeatedly declared that it would not make use of that right), and that equipment and materials ordered but not delivered by the end of the war could be acquired by the ordering country with long-term American credits. In their turn, countries entering into Lend-Lease contracts took upon themselves the obligation to render help to the United States with materials at their disposal.[54]

All in all, during the years of the war the United States made Lend-Lease deliveries to forty-two countries, amounting to nearly $50 billion dollars. In return, the U.S. received goods and services, and repayments totaling $7.4 billion dollars. Of the overall sum of Lend-Lease help, Great Britain received nearly $31 billion, France about $1.5 billion, and the national regions of China about $600 million. The entire sum of Lend-Lease deliveries to the U.S.S.R. from 1941 to 1945, according to Soviet sources, amounted to about $10 billion in war materials and other supplies,[55] approaching the $13 billion distributed to Western Europe under the post-war Marshall Plan.

After the end of World War II, there arose the problem of the terms of payments for the remaining Lend-Lease materials. In September of 1945, the U.S. discontinued Lend-Lease deliveries to the U.S.S.R. A little over a year later, in December of 1946, the United States annulled the original agreement's stipulation allowing the U.S.S.R. long-term credit for materials and equipment ordered under the Lend-Lease Agreement but not yet shipped. This unilateral annulment, claimed the Soviets, constituted a discriminatory attitude with respect to the U.S.S.R. in settling the payments under the Lend-Lease Agreement. The U.S. was also accused of delaying negotiations on the issue.[56]

In negotiations with the United States in 1947-48, 1951-52, and at the beginning of 1960, the Soviet government asserted that the Soviet Union had had the greatest effect in securing an Allied victory in World War II; therefore, Soviet diplomats argued, it could not and would not accept discriminatory measures that would leave it in a position inferior to other Lend-Lease nations. The Soviet representatives based their arguments on clauses in the Soviet-American agreement of June 11, 1942, stating that the conditions of the final settlement of the Lend-Lease Agreement should be of such a nature as to conform to the common interests of the United States of America and the Soviet Union, and further the creation and maintenance of peace in the world. The language of the pact also indicated its intention that Lend-Lease debt settlement conditions not hinder commerce, but

---

[53] Peter Petrov, "When We Were Allies," *Soviet Life*, 1991a, March issue, part 1, pp. 42-44; 1991b, May issue, part 2, pp. 18-19.

[54] *Diplomaticheskiy Slovar* [Diplomatic Dictionary], ed. A. A. Gromyko, I. I. Zemskov, V. M. Khvostov, vol. 2. Moscow: Politizdat, 1971, p. 173.

[55] Ibid., p. 174. $10 billion of Lend-Lease assistance in 1945 would be equivalent to around $130-140 billion in 2007.

[56] Ibid., p. 174.

rather encourage mutually beneficial economic relations between the two nations.[57]

Accordingly, in negotiations that took place in Washington, D.C. in January of 1960, the Soviets insisted that the agreement about the settlement of Lend-Lease matters should be reached contemporaneously with the normalization of the commercial and economic agreements between the U.S.S.R. and the U.S. However, at that time the U.S. expressed little desire to resolve the question, and the exchange of opinions between the representatives of the U.S.S.R. and the U.S. was suspended.

Although settlements were made within 15 years of the termination of the Lend-Lease programs with most of the countries that had received aid from the United States, a settlement with the U.S.S.R. would not be reached until the early 1970s, when, on October 18, 1972, an "Agreement on the Disposition of Lend-Lease Supplies in Inventory or Procurement in the United States Between the United States and the U.S.S.R." was signed.[58] In the end, the United States accepted the Soviet Union's offer to pay $722 million in installments through 2001 to settle the indebtedness. During Russian President Boris Yeltsin's visit to the United States in 1991, the parties revisited the Agreement, with the Russian government agreeing to settle the balance with a payment of $674 million to the U.S. treasury.

Looking Back and Looking Forward

Who was responsible for post-war tensions between the U.S. and the U.S.S.R.? Were they primarily a result of the Soviets' mistrust of a perceived intent on the part of the Allies to establish a "New World Order" and act as policeman of the world? The United States' influence in Asia, Europe and North Africa at the end of the war was superior to that of any other nation. The U.S. administration's interest in creating a military coalition (e.g. NATO in 1949) and in establishing military bases in strategic locations all over the world obviously attracted Stalin's attention. Did President Harry Truman misunderstand Stalin's psychological behavior at the end of the war? At the Potsdam conference in May of 1945, Truman informed Stalin of the U.S.'s intention to use nuclear weapons against Japan. In Truman's view, he was just sharing this information with his closest ally, but Stalin apparently interpreted this message as a potential threat to the Soviet socialist state. Could termination of the Lend-Lease program to the U.S.S.R. and other countries in September 1945, and Truman's approval of the "Marshall Plan" to Western Europe in 1947, have exacerbated Stalin's fears regarding U.S. post-war military expansion? In September of 1945, an American public opinion poll showed that 49 percent of Americans supported Truman's termination of the Lend-Lease program; 58 percent of the respondents believed that Lend-Lease support should be repaid in full.[59]

Or were postwar tensions a result of Soviet communist expansionist ideology, a stated part of the Marxist-Leninist agenda? Questions surrounding the causes of post-war tensions between the U.S. and U.S.S.R. are complex and must be studied objectively if we hope to elucidate the confrontational patterns between military powers in the past in order to avoid the formation of similar patterns into the future.

In the post-*Glasnost* period in Russia (after 1986), many Americans are asking the essential question: How do we build a bridge of peaceful communication with Russia and other former Soviet Republics without jeopardizing U.S. security and the world's economic and social stability? Unfortunately, there is neither a simple, concrete answer, nor a magic formula for minimizing the risk of a possible global conflict between the two nations. Up to recent times, inconsistent U.S. policies dealing with the former Soviet Union have demonstrated a lack of understanding of the Soviet people and their national values. History teaches us that nations, in some ways, are like people. While having many things in common, each is unique. As with people, a nation's behavior is often understood in terms of the psychological attitudes and style that characterize its personality. A failure to understand cultural complexity and

---

[57] Ibid., p. 174.

[58] Eduard A. Ivanyan, *Encyclopedia of Russian-American Relations (XVIII-XX Centuries)*. Moscow: International Relations, 2001, Appendix; *Timeline of Russian-American Relations 18-20th Centuries*. Embassy of the United States, Moscow, Russia.

[59] Jones, *The Roads to Russia*, p. 256.

a nation's psychological behavior in the historical context creates tension between governments and often leads to political conflict.

The history of Soviet-American relations has been quite short and somewhat intense. Evidently, President Franklin D. Roosevelt approved recognition of the Soviet Union in 1933 not out of any goodwill or political vision of peaceful cooperation with the Soviets, but for entirely pragmatic economic reasons. The Soviet Industrialization Plan required huge economic investments from the West, and in that Great Depression year of 1933 United States manufacturers needed business wherever they could find it. In fact, in the 1930s more than 200,000 unemployed Americans wrote to the Soviet Embassy in Washington, D.C., asking for work; and some of them were actually hired. Certainly, the Soviet government, in turn, hoped that diplomatic ties would open doors to United States bank loans, western technology, and the export of socialist ideology.

The post-war history of Soviet-American relations, seen from an American perspective, can be summarized as a series of Cold War cycles. The first cycle (1945-1955) might be called the Truman-Stalin duel. This period coincided with the division of Germany and Europe, the Marshall Plan, the creation of NATO, the Warsaw Treaty and the Korean War. The second cycle (1956-1973) featured Khrushchev's nuclear threat, the expansion of socialist ideology into developing countries, the development of Soviet space technology as punctuated by *Sputnik*, and the Soviet-Egyptian arms deal. The third cycle (1974-1986) began with the self-destruction of an American president, Richard Nixon, via Watergate, and the Soviet invasion of Afghanistan in 1979.[60] The United States then imposed a trade embargo, and otherwise tried to isolate the U.S.S.R. In the early 1980s, President Ronald Reagan challenged the Soviet government by increasing the U.S. nuclear and conventional military arsenal. Attempts by the Soviets to compete with the military production of the United States eventually devastated the Soviet economy, and impacted its physical environment and natural resources.

But in spite of all the mutual animosity of the Cold War, the United States and the Soviet Union never went to war against each other, fighting, at worst, by proxy. In fact, both American and Soviet leaders did a fairly good job preventing the "Hot War" between these two great nations, thereby preserving humankind for subsequent global challenges.

An analysis of the Alaska-Siberia Lend-Lease program demonstrates the need for a dynamic rather than static approach toward foreign neighbors whose political and economic systems differ from ours. The program showed that two nations could compromise in their views, and set aside conflicting cultural values and economic principles enough to achieve a common, mutually beneficial goal. A dynamic approach to dealing with potentially antagonistic neighbors, therefore, may help the United States government and United States citizens achieve favorable results in their exploration of new avenues for cultural, political, commercial and military cooperation and exchanges with Russia and the other former Soviet Republics.

---

[60] W. W. Rostow, "On Ending the Cold War," *Foreign Affairs*, vol. 65, no. 4, 1987, pp. 834-36.

The Northwest Route to Alaska

Blake W. Smith
Author/Historian
Surrey, British Columbia, Canada

Getting Started

With an August 3, 1942, agreement to transfer Lend-Lease aircraft over the Alaska-Siberia ferry route defined and formalized between the United States and the Soviet Union, plans began at once to establish a massive ferrying operation. Earliest projections called for 40 to 50 aircraft to be ferried over the route per day and the need for facilities equal to this volume. It was a bold plan, given the uncertainties involved, but reflected the Red Army's desperate need for combat planes.[1]

The Alaska-Siberia ferry route originated at a quiet and unassuming little city called Great Falls, on the western edge of the Great Plains, in Montana, chosen because of its superior year-around flying weather and geographic position at the base of a 6,000 mile-long airway that arced across northwestern Canada, Alaska and to Krasnoyarsk in Siberia — the dispersal point for aircraft headed to the battlefront.[2] *(See figure 4, page 8 of this edition.)* Landing fields were situated at roughly 200-mile intervals along the airway with facilities that ranged from modern and well equipped to roughly hacked out gravel strips void of amenities and surrounded by wilderness. Navigational aids were inadequate, weather reporting an educated flip of a coin, and detailed mapping not yet completed. The state of the Soviet portion of the route was even grimmer because of a greater number of airfields and their remote locations.

Fairbanks Handoff

By agreement, American ferry pilots were to deliver their assigned aircraft, complete with red stars emblazoned on wings and fuselage, to Fairbanks, Alaska — the designated hand-over point where the Soviets would "accept" the aircraft.[3] Upon completion of a ferry flight, an American pilot would return to Great Falls as a passenger aboard a transport plane, with the 1,900-mile trip most often made at night. Soviet pilots would continue the westward ferry flight from Fairbanks, with possible stops at Galena and a must stop at Nome before crossing the Bering Strait and hop-scotching the breadth of Siberia to Krasnoyarsk. The total distance from Fairbanks to Krasnoyarsk measured about 4,039 miles.

War in the Wilderness

The Northwest Route, as the North American portion of the Alaska-Siberia ferry route was named by the Air Transport Command (ATC), was only a partially militarized airway on the eve of Lend-Lease ferrying operations. Immediately following the December 7, 1941, Japanese attack on Pearl Harbor and America's entry into WWII, the vulnerability of the Territory of Alaska to Japanese attack became of critical concern, which led to the emergency deployment of combat aircraft over the route from the Lower Forty-eight to Alaska. The threat to Alaska was realized on June 3 and 4, 1942, when Dutch Harbor was attacked by carrier-borne planes, followed on June 6th by Japanese forces landing on

---

[1] Edwin R. Carr, *History of the Northwest Air Route to Alaska 1942-1945*, unpublished document. Historical Archives, USAF Historical Research Division, Maxwell Air Force Base, Alabama, microfilm roll #A3002, [hereinafter Carr, *History of the Northwest*], 1946, p. 59.

[2] Deane R. Brandon, "ALSIB: The Northwest Ferrying Route Through Alaska, 1942-45," *Journal of the American Aviation Historical Society*, vol. 20, no. 1, 1975, [hereinafter Brandon, ALSIB, no. 1], p. 24. The total distance Lend-Lease aircraft traveled from factories to the Russian battlefronts over the Alaska-Siberia Airway exceeded 8,000 miles.

[3] Ibid., p. 24.

and occupying two remote islands Attu and Kiska, both inhospitable outer islands along the Aleutian Chain.[4]

It was during the emergency deployment of American combat aircraft to Alaska that the Air Corps came to appreciate the hazards facing pilots flying the airway and made note of the many deficiencies that existed at isolated airfields. Beyond Edmonton, it was observed, airfields were ill-equipped to receive military aircraft in the numbers appearing—both in terms of the capacity to service aircraft and the ability to house and feed transient crews.[5] Unreliable or incomplete navigational aids and vague maps had caused some pilots to become lost, and desperately needed aircraft were destroyed in forced landings. Most notable was the loss of a flight of three B-26 bombers that were forced to belly-land in the northern wilderness, where they thereafter served the unintended duty of useful checkpoints on pilots' maps.[6]

Survey Flight
In the months preceding the August 3, 1942, formal agreement to use the Alaska-Siberia route for the purposes of aircraft ferrying, American planners—believing approval from the Soviets was likely—took steps to facilitate a large-scale ferrying operation. In light of the problems experienced in the emergency movement of aircraft, personnel, and equipment to Alaska in countering the Japanese threat to the Territory some months earlier, and appreciating that much work lay ahead in terms of airway upgrades for Lend-Lease ferrying, the Command ordered a survey to be made of the proposed route. Maj. Lloyd W. Earl, executive officer of the Northwest Sector of Ferry Command, based and headquartered at Seattle, Washington, conducted an aerial survey flight in early June.[7] Maj. Earl's orders directed that he examine all fields between Great Falls and Fairbanks and make a full report of what would be required to install fully functional air bases. On June 4, 1942, the Northwest Sector was renamed the 7th Ferrying Group.[8]

New Home and Expanded Mission
On June 20, the Commanding General of the Army Air Forces responded to the need for more centralized control of operations over the Northwest Route by placing responsibility for the route under a single agency of the Army Air Force called the Air Transport Command. Accordingly, the ATC delegated the Northwest Route functions to its own Ferrying Division, which in turn directed that the 7th Ferrying Group be moved from Seattle, Washington, to Great Falls, Montana—the new headquarters of the route.[9]

On June 22, 1942, one full year after Germany's attack on the Soviet Union, the 7th Ferrying Group closed down operations at Seattle and established its base at Great Falls. From Great Falls Municipal Airport, the 7th Ferrying Group would continue with its primary mission—the delivery of B-17 bombers from the Boeing Plant to modification centers around the U.S. Rumors began to circulate among the ranks of an expanded mission, although at this point in time no one anticipated that a massive ferrying operation of Lend-Lease aircraft to the Soviets was just around the corner. A bombing offensive against Japan from Alaska and the need to transfer aircraft up and down the route seemed the most likely shape of things to come.

Work began at once to convert Great Falls Municipal Airport into a military air base, now renamed Gore Field. While construction plans proceeded, pilots began to arrive, many having been

[4] John Haile Cloe, *Top Cover For America*. Pictorial Histories Publishing Company, 1984, p. 68.
[5] Wesley F. Craven and James L. Cate, "The Northwest Air Route to Alaska," *The Army Air Forces in World War II*, vol. VII, chapter 6. Washington D.C.: USAF Office of Air Force History, 1983, p. 155.
[6] Written correspondence with Howard J. Smiley (co-pilot aboard one of the forced-landed B-26s), dated August 16, 1999.
[7] Brandon, ALSIB, no. 1, p. 24.
[8] Ibid., p. 24.
[9] Ibid., p. 25.

reassigned from the 3rd Ferrying Group (Romulus, Michigan), and the 6th Ferrying Group (Long Beach, California), with brand new pilots assigned directly upon graduation from flight school. Enlisted men began arriving in large groups from the Army Air Force Basic Training Center at Jefferson Barracks, Missouri. In mid-July steps were taken to organize stations from Great Falls to Fairbanks, with officers and enlisted men sent north by plane, truck and train. Air bases were established or a presence added at Calgary, Edmonton, Grande Prairie, Fort St. John, Fort Nelson, Watson Lake, Whitehorse, Northway, Tanacross, Big Delta, Fairbanks, McGrath, Galena, Nome and Anchorage.[10] *(See figure 4, page 8 of this edition.)*

Group Growth

On August 1, 1942, the strength of the 7th Ferrying Group stood at 76 officers and 108 enlisted men, divided between two squadrons, the 7th Ferrying Squadron and the 25th Ferrying Squadron.[11] This force would pale in comparison to the total strength of the 7th Ferrying Group at the height of Soviet Lend-Lease ferrying, when as a mature entity the Group numbered 949 assigned officers, 17 attached officers, 1,797 assigned enlisted personnel, 30 attached enlisted personnel, 637 civilians employed at Gore Field, and 60 civilians employed at other 7th Ferrying Group installations. Of that number, the flight strength stood at 745 pilots, 32 crewmen, 50 radio operators, and 83 flight engineers. Pilots assigned to the Northern Pool—the group of pilots qualified to fly Lend-Lease aircraft over the Northwest Route—usually numbered about 100 to 160 individuals.[12] As ferrying operations matured and the ravenous demand for pilots eased, pilots were rotated in and out of the Northern Pool. Between ten and twenty delivery trips to Alaska were typical for pilots on the roster of the Northern Pool. A handful of American ferry pilots delivered over 100 aircraft. This contrasts with the duration of assignment experienced by Soviet ferry pilots, who tended to be combat pilots pulled from the front and assigned to fly one of five segments between Fairbanks and Krasnoyarsk until the ferrying mission ended. Because of their longer missions, Soviet ferry pilots conducted on average between 150 and 200 delivery flights. However, Soviet ferry pilot Peter Gamov ferried 340 bombers; Victor Perov ferried 240 fighters; Sergei Tatushin ferried 343 fighters; and Yuriy Sorokin ferried 200 bombers and 100 fighters.[13]

First Flights

The first flights by the 7th Ferrying Group from Great Falls to Alaska over the Northwest Route delivered combat aircraft to American forces in the Aleutians and flew transport flights in support of establishing air bases and other construction projects along the route. Ferry pilot Robert C. Harris recalls one memorable flight that took place during August of 1942:

> *This was the single largest flight [the] pilots of the 7th Ferrying Group had made to Alaska up to this point; twenty-one P-40s were to be delivered from San Antonio, Texas to Anchorage via Great Falls. One P-40 ended up bellied into a corn field short of Edmonton, a second landed gear-up at Fort Nelson, while a third had the gear collapse upon landing at Fairbanks.*[14]

Modest Start

The first flight of Lend-Lease aircraft bound for the Soviet Union took off from Great Falls on August 31, 1942, signaling the official commencement of a three-year ferrying mission over the Alaska-

---

[10] Ibid., p. 25.

[11] *History Of The 7th Ferrying Group, Ferrying Division, Air Transport Command.* Historical Archives, USAF Historical Research Division, Maxwell Air Force Base, Alabama, microfilm roll #A3098.

[12] Ibid.

[13] Remembrances of Peter Gamov, Yelena Makarova and Yevgemiy Radominov, a radio engineer with the Soviet Military Mission in Fairbanks between 1942-1944, offered in a joint letter dated November 16, 1991.

[14] Written correspondence with Robert C. Harris, dated August 3, 1990.

Siberia route.[15] Two flights of twin-engine Douglas A-20 bombers took off a half-hour apart, the first flight made up of four aircraft and the second of five, led respectively by Lieutenants Al Wickett and E.J. Averman. Clear weather at Great Falls gave way to thickening clouds near the Canadian border, with a cloud ceiling that descended in a stair-step progression almost to ground level. About halfway to Lethbridge, Lt. Averman spotted aircraft belonging to the earlier first flight passing below them and headed back to Great Falls. Moments later, Lt. Averman also had to turn around in the face of the deteriorating weather, and set course for a return to Great Falls.[16] About twenty minutes later, a motorist driving on a north Montana road watched as a low-flying plane, trailing flame, descended and crashed a short distance away. The motorist, John Campbell of Kevin, Montana, first to arrive at the burning wreckage, discovered the body of the pilot, twenty-two year-old Lt. Robert Gustafson, lying nearby.[17] Subsequent investigation suggested the plane struck rising terrain while in full flight. Lt. Gustafson's death marked the first casualty of the Alaska-Siberia ferrying mission.

A pair of Russia-bound Lend-Lease Douglas A-20s are dwarfed against the frozen landscape along the Northwest Route. March 8, 1943. Photo: David Greist.

Despite the tragic start to Lend-Lease ferrying over the Alaska-Siberia route, the first aircraft arrived at Fairbanks on September 3, one full month after the formal agreement to use the airway had been signed. Lt. E.J. Averman, who led the five Douglas A-20s over the Northwest Route, recalls the reception: "I remember well arriving in Fairbanks and being greeted by three Soviet representatives and one American Air Force officer. The three Soviets were very happy to see us and had a big party that evening."[18]

The first Soviets to arrive in Fairbanks as part of the Lend-Lease ferrying mission were Alexis A. Anisimov and Col. Piskunov, both representing the Soviet Purchasing Commission; they arrived on August 26. On September 3, the same day that the first flight of Lend-Lease A-20 bombers arrived, Col. Michael Machin arrived with a small group of administrative and technical personnel to lead the Soviet military mission. On September 24, the first group of Soviet ferry pilots arrived aboard transport planes.[19]

By the end of September, American ferry pilots had delivered to Fairbanks thirty Curtiss P-40 fighters and fifteen more Douglas A-20 bombers—a quantity much lower than the initial estimate of 445 that were to be delivered by month's end.[20] While aircraft gathered at Ladd Field, Soviet aircrews

[15] Brandon, ALSIB, no. 1, p. 23.

[16] Edmund J. Averman, witness statement, dated August 30, 1942, belonging to associated papers prepared by the Technical Report of Aircraft Accident Committee, dated August 31, 1942.

[17] Ibid.

[18] Written correspondence with Edmund J. Averman, dated February 24, 1999.

[19] Brandon, ALSIB, no. 1, p. 25.

[20] Carr, *History of the Northwest*, p. 66.

and technicians underwent training to familiarize themselves with the American-manufactured aircraft. American ferry pilots, with the assistance of interpreters, explained functions, procedures, and idiosyncrasies of the various aircraft types. On October 6, the first flight departed Alaska for the Soviet Union, with Lt. Col. Pavel Nedosekin leading the group of twelve A-20s.[21]

Ice in the Pipeline
As the flow of aircraft should have been increasing to a revised projected quantity of 142 planes per month, General Belyaev advised that the Siberian

Lend-Lease Douglas A-20 descending to land at Whitehorse, Yukon Territory. September 1943. Photo: Peter Collins

section of the airway was not yet ready to handle the volume of aircraft proposed.[22] This news, combined with the fact that all aircraft passing over the route after October 1 had to be winterized, added to delays that resulted in far fewer aircraft being transferred than projected. Responsibility for winterizing aircraft rested with Materiel Command and was carried out at Great Falls by the 34th Sub Depot.[23] Additional delays to aircraft deliveries were encountered throughout the three-year span of the ferry mission when the Soviets requested special modifications and servicing. Occasionally, delays would

also result from interruptions to production at the various points of manufacture. On average, an aircraft arriving at Great Falls remained within American jurisdiction for 25.3 days before handover to the Soviets at Fairbanks. After an aircraft was handed over it remained in Alaska for an average of 7.6 days before departure to Russia.[24]

Uneasy Allies
As problems began to surface during the first weeks of the ferrying mission, tensions between

Col. Machin (left), representing the Soviet Military Mission at Ladd Field, joins Col. Hart, commanding officer at Ladd Field, in greeting Col. Kiselev, chief of the Soviet mission's technical and inspection services at Ladd Field. August 1942. [Courtesy of the Magadan Civil Aviation Department]. Photo: C.E. Miller.

[21] Otis Hays, Jr., *The Alaska-Siberia Connection*. College Station: Texas A&M University Press 1996, [hereinafter Hays, *The Alaska-Siberia Connection*] p. 47. Written correspondence with Peter Gamov and (wife) Elena Makarova, dated August 29, 1992, states the date of this historic first flight into the Soviet Union, according to Gamov's flight log, as occurring on October 7, 1942; this apparent discrepancy is likely due to crossing the International Date Line.

[22] Carr, *History of the Northwest*, p. 66.

[23] Ibid., p. 66; p. 181.

[24] *Alaskan Division November 1944 – September 1945*. Historical Archives, USAF Historical Research Division, Maxwell Air Force Base, Alabama, microfilm roll #A3054.

the Americans and Soviets increased, each accusing the other of causing the delays. Beneath the veneer of goodwill and cooperation festered an ever-present rivalry between militaries, and, of course, divergent political ideologies. American President Franklin D. Roosevelt gave the highest priority to Soviet Lend-Lease shipments, and the Soviets, in a bid to ensure that same elevated status, placed key officials at all of the important points of contact between Washington, D.C. and Fairbanks to voice displeasure when impediments occurred. Elmer T. Harshbarger, who in addition to his service as a ferry pilot performed various administrative duties at Great Falls, recalls:

> *The Russians maintained (liaison) officers at all three levels of command engaged in the Lend-Lease ferrying business; Colonel Piskunov at Headquarters Air Transport Command in Washington, D.C.; Colonel Kiselev in Headquarters of the Ferrying Division of ATC at Cincinnati, Ohio; and Colonel Kotikov at the Headquarters of the 7th Ferrying Group at Great Falls, Montana. While I was Group Aircraft Maintenance Officer, Col. Kotikov was located in an office directly next to mine. We conferred almost daily on matters of movement of Russian consigned aircraft and the many problems associated with the modification and performance of the numerous types which they received. Col. Kotikov was assigned an American Army sergeant interpreter and the colonel constantly attended night school with his wife to learn English. I forget the name of the NKVD [Soviet Internal Police] official (disguised as a Russian Air Force lieutenant), who was assigned by the Russian government to keep a close watch on everything that Col. Kotikov did. It is my personal opinion that the Soviets thought he might defect. Col. Kotikov and his wife were frequent guests for dinner at our apartment. I refused to invite the guard-lieutenant, which always made him very angry indeed. I liked Col. Kotikov and noticed that he had a broad knowledge of aircraft mechanical systems and performance. We maintained a relationship of mutual respect.[25]*

Martin M. Hadacek, who arrived at Great Falls in October 1943 and remained at Gore Field until November 1945, recalls an often testy relationship between the Soviets and Americans on the flight line:

> *While stationed at Gore Field, my particular duty was working on the flight line as a mechanic maintaining aircraft that were used for transition flying (planes used for pilot training)…This [duty] also included preflight [mechanical checks] for the A-20, P-39 and C-47, which were headed to Fairbanks for the Russians. These planes had the red Russian star painted on the fuselage. If the planes were not ready for scheduled takeoff the Russian officers would really want to know what the delay was and get excited and contact higher [ranking] officers. Seemed as though they should get all the attention — or in other words, they came first.[26]*

Route Reorganization
As operational problems emerged along the Northwest Route, it became clear that having the parent organization, the 7th Ferrying Group, in the United States reduced the effectiveness of control and supervision over the airway — a situation that was especially true with respect to lagging construction projects at bases along the route, where transient aircrews slept in canvas tents and mechanics were forced to work outdoors through the winter. On October 17, 1942, the Air Transport Command addressed the situation by activating the Alaskan Wing under the command of Col. Thomas L. Mosley. Edmonton was selected as route headquarters because of its central location.[27] Seventy-three officers and 591 enlisted personnel scattered along the route and attached to the 7th Ferrying Group were absorbed into the Alaskan Wing.[28] This transfer of responsibility to the Alaskan Wing allowed the

---

[25] Written correspondence with Elmer T. Harshbarger, dated January 14, 1991.

[26] Written correspondence with Martin M. Hadacek, dated August 22, 1989.

[27] Carr, *History of the Northwest*, p. 79.

[28] Ibid.

7th Ferrying Group to focus more directly on the ferrying mission and the Alaskan Wing to exercise greater control through a period of rapid airway expansion.

Despite the reorganization, only ninety-three Lend-Lease airplanes had reached Ladd Field by the end of October. November saw the delivery of forty-eight aircraft—a number that included thirteen P-39 Airacobra fighters, a type that would prove very popular with the Soviets and lead the way as the most plentiful aircraft type delivered over the Alaska-Siberia route. As temperatures dropped with the approach of winter, so too was there a decline in aircraft deliveries, with only seven arriving during December.[29]

Snow and Ice

The concept of delivering single-engine aircraft through extreme winter climate over such a broad wilderness was untried. The Air Corps had little experience with cold weather operations and with the effects that extreme cold had on man and machine. As fate would have it, especially bitter winter temperatures settled over the Alaska-Siberia route that winter, catching most airfields minimally prepared. For personnel stationed along the airway the work was tough and the isolation could be unbearable. Every chore's difficulty was magnified by the cold. Mechanics suffered most in the cold as few hangars existed beyond Edmonton, and aircraft servicing and repair had to be done outdoors. "I found," said Maj. Elmer T. Harshbarger, a pilot and Group Aircraft Maintenance Officer based at Great Falls, "that the efficiency of mechanics working outside in below freezing and sub zero temperatures was reduced by more than half."[30] Flight engineer Corp. Rex Tanberg describes the discomfort and hazards of working in the outdoor cold, in an entry made in his wartime journal, dated February 13, 1943:

> …delivered a C-47 to Fairbanks with Maj. Winn, the temperature was minus 72 at 13:00 hrs. I froze the lobes of both my ears as I tried to drain the liquid heater system boiler on the #2 engine while it was running. They took me to hospital for attention to frostbite. They [hospital staff] were working on a young man who had tried to run from the hangar to the hospital and froze his lungs en route. He died from frozen lungs.[31]

Good Assignment

Generally, from an Army pilot's perspective, being posted to Ferry Command with the relatively passive duty of ferrying airplanes around the world was initially a disappointment. It was the passion enflamed by the Japanese attack on Pearl Harbor that had inspired many young men to enlist and become Army pilots, and many had envisioned a combat assignment.

Against the rugged backdrop of the Northwest Route a P-63A-10 cruises toward Alaska. November 1944. Photo: Lewis Wilhelm.

[29] *History of the Northwest Route, Air Transport Command.* Historical Archives, USAF Historical Research Division, Maxwell Air Force Base, Alabama, microfilm roll #A3002.

[30] Written correspondence with Elmer T. Harshbarger, dated January 14, 1991.

[31] Written correspondence with Rex Tanberg and audiotape of wartime experiences, dated September 5, 1989.

Pilots soon realized that flying the Northwest Route was serious business with little time to rest and no time to brood; besides, most came to understand that their Alaskan flights were making a tangible contribution to the war effort. The urgency of war pushed the planes forward and pilots developed a strong sense of mission, knowing the aircraft being flown would soon be in battle. Many pilots in their youth had read the stories of Jack London and the poetry of Robert Service, and saw the North through the prism of that colorful im-

A pair of Lend-Lease Bell P-39Q-20s en route *to Fairbanks over the Northwest Route. March 1944. Photo: W. Stohry.*

agery. From a pilot's winged vantage point, the Northwest Route offered spectacular scenery and exposure to adventures deep within the heart of the Yukon and Alaska—both territories rich in the history of their pioneer past. Teamwork in the air and time spent weathered-in at isolated airfields with other pilots and ground crews created a strong sense of camaraderie. Most shouldered difficulty and discomfort with good cheer, knowing that at isolated airfields permanently based ground personnel had it much worse; after all, a ferry pilot's life might find him in the sunny, warm climate of the southern regions the following week.

Two Paths
Pilots assigned to Great Falls, and the Air Transport Command (ATC) in general, came primarily from two sources. There was the pilot who enlisted in the Army and graduated from a flight training program with an aeronautical rating, and usually the rank of second lieutenant. The second source of pilots came from those trained and flying within the civilian world. These pilots offered the Air Transport Command skill and experience at a time when the military needed pilots faster than Army flying programs could produce them. Pilots from the civilian world, called "service pilots," were given the rank of Flight Officer. Both Army-trained pilots and the civilian-trained service pilots wore silver wings on their chest, but the service pilot's wings had a distinctive letter "S" inscribed on the inner shield.[32] In addition to the "militarized" civilian pilot, or service pilot, the Air Transport Command also placed a small number of civilian bush pilots on the Alaskan Wing payroll, thereby capitalizing on their local knowledge and experience. Included in this group were civilian Canadian bush pilots who found themselves in the unusual circumstance of flying U.S. military aircraft. Civilian pilots under contract generally flew the Wing's UC-64 Norseman bush planes in support of various construction projects within the Wing's jurisdiction, also taking part in search and rescue flights.

Ratings and Qualifications
The Air Transport Command rated pilots according to their qualifications, designating them Class 1 through 5. Class 1 pilots were restricted to light aircraft and primary trainers. Class 2 pilots

---

[32] Deane R. Brandon, "ALSIB: The Northwest Ferrying Route Through Alaska, 1942-45," *Journal of the American Aviation Historical Society*, vol. 20, no. 2, 1975, [hereinafter Brandon, ALSIB, no. 2], p. 106.

were restricted to flying basic and advanced single-engine trainers. Class 3 pilots were entitled to fly everything up to and including light twin-engine aircraft. Class 4 pilots were able to fly everything up to and including heavy twin-engine aircraft, such as the A-20, B-25, B-26 and C-46. Class 5, the highest rating, entitled a pilot to fly four-engine aircraft of any size and weight. In addition to any of the five classifications, a pilot qualified to fly pursuits (fighters) was denoted with the letter "P" on his qualifications record. A pilot rated "5-P" therefore had the highest qualifications and could, upon receiving a check ride, fly any aircraft. A pilot certified for instrument flight was issued a green instrument card denoting that qualification.[33]

The assembly of a core of skilled and experienced pilots was critical to the successful establishment of an efficient ferrying operation, and it came as one of the great strengths of the 7th Ferrying Group that its early nucleus was formed by skimming highly qualified pilots from other ferrying groups, principally the 6th Ferrying Group based at Long Beach, California. These pilots, who had joined the Air Corps before the war, established policies and procedures for flights over the Northwest Route that would, over time, save many lives.

Mixed Bag

During the early winter of 1942-43, when the flow of Lend-Lease aircraft was but a trickle, ferry pilots assigned to the northern run were engaged primarily in shuttling U.S. military aircraft to and from

Alaska. Typically, a ferry pilot might deliver a factory new Lend-Lease airplane to Ladd Field and expect a speedy return to Great Falls aboard a transport plane. Sometimes, however, orders would be received upon landing to ferry one of the Eleventh Air Force's war-weary combat planes back to Great Falls—planes that were often runout or in need of special repairs stateside. Usually, these return flights originated from Anchorage's Elmendorf Field, the main base of operations for the Eleventh Air Force. A transport plane was available to shuttle ferry pilots between Ladd Field and Elmendorf Field for purposes such as this. Another common diversion experienced by ferry pilots occurred when they received orders to test fly and deliver aircraft that

Bell P-63 Kingcobra in flight over the Northwest Route with inscription written in chalk on its fuselage reading "Bell Booby Trap," so named because the Bell planes, held up for mechanical repairs and delayed for extended periods of time in the outdoor cold, tended to be involved in a greater number of crashes than other aircraft. May 1945.

had been delayed along the route for mechanical repair. The repairs might take weeks to complete, so the original pilot would have long since been shuttled back to Great Falls to resumed ferrying duties.

---

[33] Ibid., p. 106.

Bell's P-39 Airacobra and P-63 Kingcobra fighters were nicknamed "Bell Booby Traps." Because repairs of these planes were so time-consuming, and their crash rates so disproportionately high, pilots handled them with extra caution. After orders for the onward delivery of these mechanically-delayed aircraft had been cut in Great Falls, generally the more experienced pilots were assigned as "mop-up pilots" to retrieve them.

Survival Gear

When cold weather set in over the Northwest Route in mid-October 1942, ferry pilots had yet to be supplied with warm winter flight gear, so most wore their summer uniforms and took along a heavy jacket. Even survival kits were not included as "must carry" items by ferry pilots leaving Great Falls; it was up to an individual pilot to put together his own kit. At the time, the Army Air Force had little experience with flight into cold weather regions and was neither prepared for nor fully appreciative of the hazards facing pilots forced down in the northern wilderness—in summer or winter.

Though flying into winter weather ill-equipped sparked much concern among pilots, it seemed low on the scale of priority with Wing headquarters staff; their attention was absorbed by many other pressing issues in the early stages of the ferrying mission. Lack of winter flight gear finally did draw Alaskan Wing attention following a November 5, 1942, forced landing in the Yukon wilds just east of Wellesley Lake. The mishap occurred when ferry pilot Lt. Pennington became separated from others in flight and was forced by a sputtering engine to land his P-36 on an open patch of snow. Pennington spent two days with his wrecked aircraft in temperatures that dipped as low as 30° C below zero before he was located and rescued. Fortunately, Lt. Pennington survived the mishap, thanks in part to the heavy coat he wore. But his feet suffered severe frostbite. Upon learning of the mishap, Brigadier General Dale V. Gaffney, the no-nonsense commander of Ladd Field's Cold Weather Testing Detachment, grew angry over the circumstances that precipitated the forced landing, and questioned why Pennington himself was not more proactive in his bid to survive—he had not lit and maintained a fire or otherwise attempted to make a signal to alert searchers.

Land and Live in the Arctic

An inquiry into the mishap was held at Great Falls during late December, with Maj. Ponton de Arce, commander of the 7th Ferrying Group presiding.[34] After interviews were conducted and all aspects of the forced landing examined, a multi-page directive was issued to pilots outlining new procedures and policies aimed at ensuring their greater safety when flying over the Northwest Route. Important new guidelines made it a requirement that pilots be issued and carry an "Arctic Kit" on all flights; this kit, which formed a part of the seat-pack portion of the parachute, contained various survival items, including, among other things, matches, a hatchet, snare wire, food items, fishing line and hooks, a pair of gloves, a wool face mask, flares and a flare gun. It was also made a requirement that pilots be issued appropriate winter clothing and insulated boots, and that before a pilot could make a flight over the route he be required to receive instruction on wilderness survival. A film was made to be shown during training sessions titled *Land and Live in the Arctic*, with popular entertainer Bob Hope narrating. The clincher at the film's end was a close up shot of Lt. Pennington's black and blue feet, minus several toes.

Ferry pilot Robert C. Harris, who joined the Ferry Command as a civilian pilot and made his first flight to Alaska in August 1942, comments on the early state of flight preparation:

> We had an excellent survival training film but it took months to get proper boots and clothing to survive an emergency landing. We were [on November 5, 1942] bringing 5 planes [3 P-36s and 2 P-38s] to Great Falls that had been in the Aleutians. One of the P-36s had engine failure and landed on a frozen lake south of Northway. The pilot survived and was rescued. He was wearing the short

---

[34] Statement and transcript of inquiry provided by Frank McClure (one of the principals involved in the Pennington mishap), dated December 29, 1942, forwarded September 16, 1993.

fur-lined boots, regular issue. Snow got into the boots, melted and froze, and the pilot lost three toes...high-top boots were issued soon after.[35]

Leading the Way

Though the concept of making flights over the route in groups of two or more planes was informally practiced in the early going, particularly when flying single-engine aircraft, the notion of safety in numbers was formalized as a result of the Pennington mishap, in a directive ordering that:

ferrying of single-engine aircraft over the Northern Route will be in groups. Only under exceptional circumstances will an aircraft be cleared alone. The circumstances are: 1) That a pilot of the aircraft is qualified as a flight leader. 2) That there is a good indication that there will be no flight over the station for three days to which the aircraft could join. 3) If a flight is at another station, this aircraft may be cleared alone to that station for the purposes of joining that flight providing weather is unquestionably CFR [Contact Flight Rules – minimums of 3-mile visibility and 1,000-foot ceilings]. The clearing alone of twin-engine aircraft which do not carry a co-pilot, such as A-20s and P-38s, will be discouraged, as bad weather and terrain are not conducive to the safe, solo operation of these aircraft.[36]

A flight leader was a pilot who had made at least several trips over the Northwest Route, selected on the basis of having sufficient skills relating to navigation and formation flying, and who was fully familiar with safety and survival procedures. As the route matured and new ferry pilots began arriving in large numbers, the need for flight leaders resulted in the establishment of a school at Great Falls for the purpose. Ferry pilot Lt. Stephen Van Nostrand, who helped start the school, recalls,

After making about twenty or thirty trips north, I was selected to set up a school at Great Falls to train flight leaders whose job would be to shepherd new pilots over the route to Alaska. The flight leader school was thought to be the best answer to produce a large number of competent flight leaders able to meet the huge volume of planes going through to Russia...at the end of the ground school part in Great Falls, I would have the prospective new flight leader take off – just he and I – him leading, me on his right wing, staying close enough for me to see hand signals and communicate.[37]

Upon successful completion of the ground school and check flight, a pilot was declared a certified flight leader. For pilots of pursuit-type aircraft attached to a flight leader as a wingman it was important to hold a position in the formation, close or wide, in such a manner that the pilot of the lead plane could easily see all ships in his formation. A change of position or sudden absence of a flight member would alert the flight leader of trouble and initiate actions to assist the pilot. Former ferry pilot Sam Burgess affirms that single-engine aircraft flights were:

always with at least one other aircraft for safety in case you had to bail out [then] someone could mark your position and call for rescue...however, some wingmen would drift away to "sightsee" but this was taking a chance. A good wingman always flies so the flight leader can see him out of the corner of his eye.[38]

Flight Time

The distance from Great Falls to Fairbanks represented about 1,900 air miles, or between nine and fourteen hours of flying time in pursuit-type aircraft. Delivery time could range from one day with

---

[35] Written correspondence with Robert C. Harris, dated August 3, 1990.

[36] *Alaskan Division: November 1942 – October 1944.* Historical Archives, USAF Historical Research Division, Maxwell Air Force Base, Alabama, microfilm roll #A3053.

[37] Written correspondence with Stephen Van Nostrand and audiotape of wartime experiences, dated March 31, 1999.

[38] Written correspondence with Sam Burgess, dated May 30, 1991.

Lend-Lease Douglas A-20s at Ladd Field awaiting delivery into Russia. April 12, 1943. Photo: USAF via Blake W. Smith.

three landings, to three weeks and ten landings. Primary factors influencing delivery time included mechanical difficulties, seasonal daylight availability, and weather conditions *en route*. Only during the summer months when the hours of daylight were sufficient did the single-engine pilots complete a delivery flight to Fairbanks in a single day. During the northern winter, when daylight hours were few, simply making the next landing field could be a day's objective.

The Road North

Arrival at Edmonton signaled the "gateway" to the North and the beginning of the wilderness portion of the Northwest Route. The Alaskan Wing directed that all northbound flights stop at Edmonton unless they had special permission to bypass the base, in which case a mandatory radio check was required. Since Edmonton was home to Alaskan Wing Headquarters, it served as a clearinghouse for communications along the airway, and messages to aircrews were often passed on during this required stop. As at all stops *en route* to Alaska it was incumbent upon a pilot to check weather forecasts and top up gasoline tanks before continuing. Since pilots of single-engine aircraft were restricted to contact flight (Visual Flight Rules—VFR), certain visual references or check points were important when flying over such a vast wilderness. In March of 1942, construction began on the Alaska Highway, one of the great engineering triumps of the twentieth century, connecting Dawson Creek, British Columbia, with Big Delta, Alaska. For a distance of almost 1,600 miles the airway loosely followed the thin dirt road, and pilots flying "contact" always kept a mental note of whether the road lay off the left wing or the right wing. "We pilots depended on that cut of highway time and time again," recalls ferry pilot Carl H. Biron. "It was a navigational asset and a security blanket in times of bad weather or engine/mechanical failure."[39] Lt. Frank E. Calhoun found himself among ferry pilots thankful for the highway's proximity to their flight path when, on May 16, 1943, his P-39 lost power while descending to land at Watson Lake airfield, forcing him to set down on the new road. Calhoun survived the highway landing and

---

[39] Written correspondence with Carl H. Biron, dated September 15, 1989.

flagged down a passing army truck that in turn delivered him to Watson Lake.[40] Almost a year later, on May 5, 1944, another 7th Ferrying Group pilot was grateful for a stretch of Alaska Highway. On this occasion Lt. Jimmie L. Fields was ferrying a war-weary P-39 from the Aleutians to Great Falls when his engine lost power while over the rugged mountains of the Wolf Range. Fields spotted a stretch of road and crash-landed the plane without injury.[41]

Three of the four approaches to land at the Watson Lake military airdrome were over water. View is over the nose of a Lend-Lease B-25 Mitchell on approach to land. May 1945. Photo: Kenneth Miller.

Help Wanted

The Alaska-Siberia ferry operation would get off to a slow start in the fall of 1942, largely due to the haste with which the daring and ambitious plan had been conceived and set into motion. Among the impediments to establishing an efficient ferry route were the extreme winter climate, and the tremendous distances to be traversed. *En route* airfields were primitive, undermanned and ill equipped to perform the mission that lay before them, and required resources were hotly competed for within other theaters of operation. A shortage of ferry pilots was especially acute through the first months of the ferrying operation; but, in January of 1943, new pilots began arriving at Great Falls in a small but steady stream. Many of these pilots were fresh from flight school and assigned with others from their graduating class *en masse*. The largest airplane most had flown was the T-6, a two-place trainer that was the standard "last step" before the jump-up to the types they would be delivering to the Soviets. A variety of aircraft were kept at Great Falls for the sole purpose of training pilots.

Typically, a newcomer to the 7th Ferrying Group might have about 200 total flying hours upon graduating from flight school. Transition training, as checking out on a certain type of plane was called, consisted of little more than a quick ground briefing while sitting in the cockpit. A pilot would take off and land several times before being declared ready to go. Ferry pilot Sam Burgess, who joined the 7th Ferrying Group in November of 1942, recalled, "If you thought you could fly it — have at it — that was the name of the game. My instructor in the P-39 had [a total of] three landings and takeoffs the day before."[42] "We got a walk around the aircraft, a cockpit check, and a pat on the back," recalls ferry pilot Bill Wise.

We were on our own from the first takeoff, and did we love it. We had been well-trained — we truly thought we could "fly the boxes they came in!" Eager is the only adjective that would apply. We couldn't wait to fly the most powerful aircraft we had ever seen. And after we flew it, our only question was: Which way is Fairbanks?[43]

[40] Written correspondence with Frank E. Calhoun, dated September 11, 1990.

[41] Written correspondence with Leslie Hiderman (Jimmie L. Fields' daughter), dated October 13, 1999.

[42] Written correspondence with Sam Burgess, dated May 30, 1991.

[43] Blake W. Smith, *Warplanes to Alaska: The story of a WWII military supply lifeline to Alaska and Russia through the Canadian wilderness.* Surrey, B.C.: Hancock House Publishers, 1998, p. 115; written correspondence with Bill Wise, dated April 13, 1991.

Bent Birds

Pilot inexperience and youthful enthu-
siasm, combined with the competitive
nature of the fighter pilot, often led to accidents involving poor judgment, with
planes wrecked and pilots killed. The record shows that P-39 and P-63-type aircraft accounted for the highest propor-
tion of accidents, with one out of every
forty-four P-39s meeting with some form
of mishap between Great Falls and Fairbanks, and one out of every thirty-seven
P-63s running into some kind of trouble.
Pilot error topped the list of causes for
P-39 accidents, while mechanical failure
led the causes of P-63 mishaps, with pilot error rating a close second. Failing to
turn back in the face of poor weather conditions was a common cause of accidents
away from airports; this led to numerous
incidents of pilots striking the ground in
full flight or becoming lost and forced to
land on a frozen lake, or to bail out over
wild and unfamiliar territory.

When an airplane was reported over-
due or was known to have gone down, a
search was initiated using locally available Alaskan Wing aircraft, such as the
UC-64 Norseman bush plane or twin-engine Beech AT-11 and C-47 transports.
Within Canadian territory, in addition
to Wing aircraft, the Royal Canadian Air
Force (RCAF) contributed planes and pilots, and, occasionally, training aircraft
and crews from Number 2 Air Observa-

7th Ferrying Group pilots Bill Wise and Wayne Watson (in cockpit) pose for snapshot upon landing at Watson Lake airfield. April 1943. Photo: Wayne Watson.

tion School based at Edmonton. Such was the case on February 6, 1943, when foul winter weather
had planes and crews grounded along the Northwest Route waiting for snowstorms to blow through.
Col. Mensinger, the operations officer at Wing headquarters in Edmonton, was among the weather-
grounded at Watson Lake waiting for clearance for a return to Edmonton as a passenger aboard a C-49
transport. Later that day, after clearance was issued, Mensinger's plane departed in a swirl of ice crys-
tals for points south. Also that day a C-47 came in on an instrument approach to land at Watson Lake
during the height of a snow storm, miscalculated his landing, and applied power for a go-around and
another try. Both airplanes disappeared. Search aircraft were called in, including five RCAF training
aircraft from Edmonton, joined briefly by Lend-Lease P-39s to fly search sorties. The C-47 was found
nineteen days later, just four miles off the end of the runway in heavily wooded terrain. The pilot and
co-pilot had been killed in the crash, but two passengers were rescued; both had broken legs and had
endured temperatures of 35° C below zero. After two months of intensive searching, Col. Mensinger's
C-49 and the eleven men on board were declared lost. It was not until September of 1948 that the
wreckage was discovered at the base of a jagged peak near Fort St. John. All aboard had perished

instantly.[44] Both losses illustrate well the challenges such a vast wilderness presented in searching for downed planes.

Search and Rescue

Oddly, search and rescue was slow to organize along the Northwest Route and it was not until mid-January 1944 that crews, planes, and equipment were dedicated for that exclusive purpose. Flight surgeons received training to parachute to downed airmen in need of immediate aid and render assistance in moving the victim to a location accessible to air or ground evacuation. Another innovative rescue technique was to attach dogs to parachute harnesses so that they could accompany the flight surgeons on para-rescue missions. These dogs, called "para-pups," were selected from strong northern breeds and rigged with saddle-bag-type packs able to carry between 35 and 50 pounds of gear. Those involved in the training claim that the dogs offered no resistance to being tossed out of the Norseman bush plane and descended in their parachutes completely relaxed, landing without difficulty.[45]

An example of a successful para-rescue operation occurred on May 1, 1944, when P-39 pilot Lt. Marcello J. Sommovigo was forced to bail out of his burning plane south of Fort Nelson. Fortunately Lt. Sommovigo was able to radio his situation and location to Fort Nelson moments before he parachuted from his stricken ship. Fort Nelson's search and rescue unit sprang into action with para-rescue flight surgeon Capt. Jacobs parachuting to the aid of the injured pilot and treating the downed flyer's burns on scene within an hour. Jacobs spent the night in a makeshift camp with Lt. Sommovigo and the following morning both men were evacuated by floatplane from a nearby river.[46]

Cutting Loose

Low flying or "buzzing" was a common practice among ferry pilots, many viewing the adrenaline rush it produced as a welcome interlude from the tedium endured through long hours spent flying from one base to another. Some flight leaders did not encourage any form of aerial horseplay, "however, there were those who did," recalls service pilot Andrew Traverso, who made forty flights to Alaska. "All the time I was flight leader I would never permit it. I am sure a few accidents were due to just that." [47] Ferry pilot Ben L. Brown, who participated in buzzing, recalls:

> After a few trips north we began to know most of the personnel at the various bases en route and knew pretty much what we could get away with regarding buzzing, low-altitude aerobatics and the like…There were accidents and a few guys got killed, but fortunately none in the flights I led.[48]

Among the buzzing mishaps that gained the most notoriety was an April 15, 1943, crash of a P-39 that was being flown on a local test hop by Lt. Frank Grayson at Whitehorse. Grayson attempted to dazzle a handful of onlookers with a low altitude roll while over the main runway; unfortunately the nose of the P-39 dipped and struck the runway, causing the airplane to explode. Grayson was killed. A little over a month later, on May 18, 1943, two P-39 pilots left Great Falls with Lt. R.E. Gillen leading Lt. Robert W. Peters. While over the prairie farmland of southern Alberta, Gillen led Peters in a high-speed dive and subsequent low swooping pass over Keho Lake. Lt. Peter's propeller and belly fuel tank contacted the lake's surface, causing the plane to skip into the air, rotate into an inverted position,

---

[44] "Eleven Skeletons Brought Out by Pack Train From U.S.A.F. Plane Wrecked In '43." *Alaska Highway News,* September 30, 1948.

[45] Blake W. Smith, *Warplanes to Alaska.* Surrey, B.C.: Hancock House Publishers, 1998, p. 179; Written correspondence with Robert Stribbling, Alaskan Division of Search & Rescue based at Whitehorse during WWII, dated November 28, 1999.

[46] Written correspondence with Marcello J. Sommovigo, dated February 12, 1999.

[47] Written correspondence with Andrew Traverso, dated February 6, 1988.

[48] Written correspondence with Ben L. Brown, dated April 29, 1999.

and crash nose-down into the lake—plane and pilot disintegrating within a towering plume of spray. Later that summer, on July 24, 1943, a Lend-Lease Douglas A-20 piloted by Lt. Carl R. Holben struck some trees on the approach perimeter at Teslin airfield and exploded in a fireball that stretched the length of the runway. The mishap claimed the lives of Lt. Holben and his passenger flight engineer Sgt. Carl E. Schultz. Witnesses said Holben was buzzing the airfield and misjudged his altitude, resulting in the fatal accident.[49]

Gaffney Takes Charge

In the spring of 1943 the flow of Lend-Lease aircraft steadily increased as warmer weather shifted the focus away from surviving the winter to completing the mission at hand. Air base construction projects could resume or begin as the snow receded and long-lost materials reappeared from under a thick mat of winter snow. Aircraft hangers and other important buildings resumed construction at all bases, promising life would be much easier and the ferrying mission more streamlined going into subsequent winters. On May 9, 1943, General Dale V. Gaffney, former commander of Ladd Field's Cold Weather Testing Detachment, was named the commander of the Alaskan Wing, replacing Col. Thomas L. Mosley, who had been in charge of the Wing since it was activated on October 17, 1942.[50] Col. Mosley was reassigned to oversee ATC operations in North Africa.

Much work lay ahead, and Gaffney, who had a reputation for being a hard-nosed whip-cracker and who possessed the nickname "Screaming Eagle of the Yukon," was undoubtedly the man for the job. Gaffney's experience as commander of Ladd Field's Cold Weather Testing Detachment meant that he was familiar with the ferrying mission and the various airway projects and challenges involved. Under his command the flow of aircraft steadily increased on a month over month basis until a peak of 403 deliveries was reached for the single month of August 1944.[51] Delivery totals would remain high through the remainder of the ferry mission, with the exception of October 1944, when the Soviets refused to accept any more of the newly introduced P-63 Kingcobra fighters until special strengthening modifications to the rear fuselage had been completed. Around-the-clock work resulted in this task being finished by November, when the steady flow resumed.[52]

Gaffney was also charged with overseeing and accelerating the pace of airbase improvements and numerous construction projects along the airway. In little over a year Gaffney was able to race the majority of these projects to completion, and under his command the route matured and the airway achieved a high standard of efficiency. Much of this work had to be done while maintaining international relationships amid complex issues that arose with an airway and mission involving three countries—the United States of America, the Soviet Union, and Canada.

Friends and Allies

Since the majority of the Northwest Route traversed Northwestern Canada, the important issue of Canadian sovereignty arose with the massive flood of U.S. troops onto Canadian territory. It was partly with this in mind that the RCAF operated and maintained the airfields on Canadian soil, a commitment the RCAF, thinly-stretched because of overseas manning commitments, was challenged to fulfill. At airfields located in Calgary, Edmonton, Grande Prairie, Fort St. John, Fort Nelson, Watson Lake, and Whitehorse, the U.S. Army was also present as functioning air base units, often in numbers that exceeded their RCAF hosts.[53] Gen. Gaffney, though headquartered at Edmonton, traveled frequently over the airway to confer with the RCAF. Insight into this relationship is offered by the

---

[49] *Alaskan Division: November 1942 – October 1944.* Historical Archives, USAF Historical Research Division, Maxwell Air Force Base, Alabama, microfilm roll #A3053.

[50] Carr, *History of the Northwest*, p. 86.

[51] Ibid., p. 199.

[52] Ibid., p. 200.

[53] U.S.A.F. personnel were also stationed at the following Canadian airfields that fell within the jurisdiction of the Alaskan Division: Lethbridge, Fort McMurray, Fort Simpson, Dawson Creek, Fort Smith, Norman Wells, Camp Canol, Prince George.

RCAF's Northwest Command Headquarters (Edmonton) daily journal entry dated July 31, 1943:

> *Constant liaison with the USAAF has been maintained and the most cordial of relationships exist. Certain fears have been held by the H.Q. that the RCAF "hold" on the Route was slipping because of ambitious plans of the USAAF. However, these fears are now banished as the result of recent intimations that action would be taken to place the RCAF in a more advantageous position.*[54]

Points of friction exasperated Gaffney on occasion, but by and large the relationship with Canadian officials and the RCAF was mutually respectful, with both sides working together to resolve issues as they arose. The Soviet-American relationship, into which Gen. Gaffney entered as a central figure, proved much more complex, with undercurrents of suspicion pervading nearly every interaction. The Soviets had, as Gen. John R. Deane, chief of the United States Military Mission to Moscow (1942-45), described, "an inherent [historical] distrust of foreigners and may be expected to examine for a hidden motive any proposal for collaboration."[55] The Alaska-Siberia ferry mission was too important in the cooperative battle to defeat Nazi Germany to allow political, economic, or language differences to sabotage its effectiveness as a delivery

American ferry pilot (left) is greeted by a Soviet representative at Ladd Field upon delivery of a Lend-Lease P-39 Airacobra that was purchased by subscription and presented as a gift from School 51, Buffalo, New York. May 1943. Photo: USAF via Blake W. Smith.

method. To overcome these obstacles, liaison officers fluent in both languages and cultures helped calm various crises as they developed.

Officers of the Soviet Military Mission appeared to appreciate services done by American crews, but made little effort to establish friendships with their American hosts. American personnel at Nome and Fairbanks, the usual points of contact with the Soviets, were aware that their Soviet counterparts were under orders not to fraternize. It was generally known too that NKVD (People's Commissariat of Internal Affairs) spies hovered where intermingling might occur, ensuring the Soviets' strict observance of those orders.

Contact between American and Soviet ferry pilots was usually restricted to a nod and possibly a smile on Ladd Field or on a sidewalk in Fairbanks. Establishing friendships was difficult because of the language barrier and also because flight schedules kept everyone on the move. Weeks or possibly months might pass before seeing one another again at Ladd Field.

---

[54] *North West Staging Route, North West Air Command: June 6, 1942 – October 31, 1945.* RCAF daily activities and reports on microfilm reel #C-12164, Public Archives of Canada.

[55] Hays, *The Alaska-Siberia Connection*, p. 25.

Ferry pilot Malcolm J. Maheu, who made his first northern flight in January 1945 and subsequently delivered six P-63s to Ladd Field, recalls his first reception at Ladd Field: "Russian pilots attempted to break up our landing approach . . . we were warned of this and kept a tight formation. They did fly across the runway, just ahead of us as we were touching down." Maheu recalls that when he met Soviet pilots, most often in the tunnel connecting the PX with the mess hall,

> *...they were mostly in groups of two or more and recognition was seldom given. In the mess hall they chose a table to themselves. I always thought they had strict orders to avoid us. The only time I ever noticed any change in expression was when they were purchasing merchandise in the PX...*[56]

The impression most American ferry pilots formed of their Soviet counterparts was that they tended to look older, were shorter and stockier, drank a lot of vodka, and tended to fly recklessly. Elliott Tremaine remembers:

> *We drank with the Russian pilots in the officers' club at Fairbanks. They were all young like we were and they tended to be reckless. Several of them were killed trying to slow-roll on takeoff. When I questioned the wisdom of this maneuver their response was "are you afraid to die?"*[57]

Occasionally, Soviet and American pilots drank together at the officers' club or at a downtown bar; the Americans preferring beer, the Russians vodka. Ferry pilot Carl H. Biron recalls:

> *...on occasion we would drink vodka and shoot pool with the Russian pilots and found them to be excellent shootists and quite capable of handling large quantities of vodka. Usually we would be furnished a Russian-speaking interpreter. All of this kind of contact went on at Ladd Field.*[58]

Wing Becomes Division

The manpower strength of the Alaskan Wing steadily increased under Gaffney's command and by the summer of 1944 most of the hazards and discomforts that were the cause of the route's early reputation had been tamed. Heated hangars offered refuge from the cold for mechanics and servicing crews. Gone were the canvas tents. Pilots and ground-based personnel slept in reasonably warm quarters, some with hot showers, and the mess offered good food. In addition to enjoying greater comforts and conveniences on the ground, pilots could look beneath their wings while

Soviet airman examines the Wright Double Cyclone R-2600 engine of a Douglas A-20 as part of his pre-flight check before ferrying the airplane into Russia. Photo: USAF via Blake W. Smith.

---

[56] Written correspondence with Malcolm J. Maheu, dated March 7, 1991.

[57] Written correspondence with Elliott Tremaine, dated August 6, 1988.

[58] Written correspondence with Carl H. Biron, dated September 15, 1989.

in flight and see a series of intermediate emergency air strips reaching completion at mid-way points between the major landing fields, offering a landing spot in case of trouble. Life was not easy with so much work to be done, but conditions were much more bearable than those endured previously.

On July 1, 1944, as part of the worldwide administrative reorganization of the ATC, the Alaskan Wing became the Alaskan Division.[59] About thirty bases were brought under the control of the Alaskan Division, from Great Falls to Nome and to the tip of the Aleutians. A system of rotation was implemented whereby personnel stationed in the North could move around the Division or elsewhere within the ATC. November 1944 brought a peak strength of almost 10,000 personnel in the Division. From then on, a gradual decline would occur until the cessation of hostilities.[60]

Mission Accomplished

During the spring of 1945, events on the world stage moved quickly as Allied forces advanced steadily into the heart of Germany. On April 12, U.S. President Franklin D. Roosevelt passed away after a period of illness. When Vice President Harry S. Truman assumed the presidency he found himself in the position of having to make some of history's most difficult decisions, including the decision to drop atomic bombs on Japan. On April 30, Hitler perished at his own hand as German resistance collapsed, and, on May 8th, Germany surrendered. On May 12, President Truman announced the cancellation of the Lend-Lease program to the Soviets. Stalin was deeply annoyed by the unilateral decision because he believed he had assurance that aid would continue until Japan had been defeated. Stalin himself had pledged during the Yalta Conference the previous February to enter the war against Japan within three months of Germany's surrender. After a flurry of diplomatic wrangling, American officials clarified that Lend-Lease aid destined to prosecute war against Germany would cease, but shipments aimed at the defeat of Japan would continue.[61]

The end of hostilities in Europe created a very unclear picture along the Northern Route as to the future of Lend-Lease aircraft transfers. Gone was the urgency that had characterized the early days of the ferrying mission, when the outcome of the war teetered in the balance, and the notion that Lend-Lease aircraft being delivered over the Alaska-Siberia airway might tip that balance toward Soviet victory. Now, even the normally hard-driven Soviet pilots were observed to be uncharacteristically at ease, and aircraft transferred to their control began to stack up at Fairbanks and Nome for want of onward delivery.[62]

Aircraft commitments to the Soviets shifted to a wind-down schedule, as nearly all aircraft types that had become a familiar sight along the route neared the end of their runs. The exception was the appearance for the first time of AT-6 training aircraft, 225 of which were slated for delivery, and the continuation of C-47 transport deliveries, with 240 to be delivered at a rate of forty per month until the end of the year.[63]

On August 6, 1945, the Japanese city of Hiroshima was nearly leveled by a single atomic bomb dropped by an American B-29 bomber, followed on August 9 by a second atomic bomb dropped with similar effect on the Japanese city of Nagasaki. Japan quickly capitulated and on August 14 at 4:00 p.m. word was wired up and down the Northern Route that the war was over.[64] Lend-Lease aircraft transfers were immediately halted and the twenty aircraft *en route* ordered to return to Great Falls.

---

[59] A Division being the highest unit of command in the ATC, followed by the Wing, then the Army Air Base. A Division may have one or more Wings (*North Star, Alaskan Wing, Air Transport Command Newspaper*, dated July 31, 1944.).

[60] Carr, *History of the Northwest*, p. 97.

[61] Hays, *The Alaska-Siberia Connection*, p. 127.

[62] Brandon, ALSIB, no. 2, p. 109.

[63] Carr, *History of the Northwest*, p. 203.

[64] *RCAF Station Watson Lake*. RCAF daily activities and reports on microfilm reel #C-12.208, Public Archives of Canada.

U.S.S.R. There were numerous of losses along this route and it was difficult to carry large armaments on regular transportation vessels. The route across the Pacific to the Far East ports was inconvenient and too long. The Indian Ocean route via the port of Basra, Iraq, on the Persian Gulf, to Iran, and on to the Soviet borders was initially thought to be the best main transportation artery; however, it was also a very long and inconvenient route due to its many trans-shipment points. Nevertheless, the Indian Ocean route played an important role in the delivery of necessary cargo to the Soviet Union. None of these routes, however, would prove suitable for transportation of fragile and cumbersome aircraft.

Searching for an Airway Route

In July of 1941, the U.S.S.R. State Committee of Defense (SCD) decided to build a special air route to connect the Soviet Union to the United States. V.S. Molokov, head of the Central Board (Headquarters) of the U.S.S.R. Civil Aviation, and a well-known polar pilot, led the search for a possible air route. On Molokov's order, a group of prominent aviation specialists traveled to West Siberia, Yakutia, and

Pilot V.I. Kuzmin, Yakut-native pilot. Courtesy of Ivan Negenblya.

Chukotka to search for a route. After comprehensive analyses of several alternatives, they chose a route via the Bering Strait, to the central regions of Chukotka, Yakutia, and on to Krasnoyarsk. The advantages of this route over the others was that it maintained prevailing stable anticyclone weather and contained relatively large settlements that divided the route into several, almost equal, sections. Significantly, the Trans-Siberian Railway passed through Krasnoyarsk, the terminus of the route in West Siberia. An additional attraction was that parts of the route were well explored and had been flown previously by civil aviation crews.[4]

The SCD ordered leaders from the head office of Civil Aviation and East Siberian economic organizations to supply all necessary materials and manpower to construct the airway, and to accomplish it in the shortest time possible. D.E. Chucov was placed in charge of the 4,913 km route [from Uelkal to Krasnoyarsk]. Having formerly headed up the Planning and Economic Section of the Main Department of Civil Aviation and also having worked in the East-Siberian Department of Civil Aviation, D.E. Chucov knew the area well. Initially, an expedition was undertaken to search for suitable airfield sites. V.S. Molokov recalled that it was only from the air that the search team managed to find the proper spot in Oymyakon. In the swampy region of the Omolon River, a tributary of the Kolyma River, two members of the expedition parachuted in to find a place where the American U-2 (Utility) airplane could land.

During the planning and searching process, it became apparent that it was necessary to change the initially planned route. The final point of the route was originally planned to be Anadyr, but there was no suitable place for an airport. The tundra was too swampy. Uelen couldn't be used either because analysis of weather reports revealed that the spot was too often covered by fog. Ultimately, the settlement of Uelkal, situated on the shore of the Gulf of Anadyr (Chukotka), was chosen as the final point of the Siberian route. For additional safety, it was decided that an alternate airfield, 200 km off the final point of the route, in Markovo, would be built.[5]

---

[4] I. P. Mazuruk, "Vozdushny most Alaska-Sibir," [The Air Route Alaska-Siberia], *Polyarny Krug*, 1978. Moscow: Mysl, 1978, p. 53.

[5] V.S. Molokov, *Rodnoye Nebo* [The Home Sky], 2nd edition. Moscow: Voyenizdat, 1987, pp. 99, 100.

V. I. Kuzmin, one of the first Yakut-native pilots, transported the team that searched for the route. Sometimes the transports took place on a U-2, and other times he used the larger P-5 plane. According to Kusmin:

> *The work proved to be difficult and exerted all our efforts. Together with the exploring specialists and designers, the crews had been circling over the vast unknown taiga and mountain hills stretching from Yakutsk to the Bering Straits. We were to complete the research work for the new air route within four months — the term established by the government.*
>
> *Having landed on the ground chosen from the air, the pilots took axes and together with all the workers went to cut down the trees and to do other manual work.*
>
> *Almost after each landing, the aircraft needed careful inspection and some repairs. They had to perform ten or more difficult landings a day. In spring, when the daylight time became longer, they flew 8-10 hours a day.*
>
> *The explorers had been going deeper and deeper into the hardly accessible regions. Across the Aldan River, along the route to Chukotka, the mountainous area began, where, in spite of beginning of spring, there was still severe cold. They spent the night where they worked; long before the dawn the pilots had to come out of the sleeping bags and frozen tents into the biting frost and piercing wind. The preparation and warming up of the aircraft with facilities available at that time demanded high skills, know how, and participation of the pilots and mechanics.*[6]

Building the Airfields on the Uelkal-Krasnoyarsk Route

In a short period of time, the tundra and *taiga* sites selected by the reconnaissance teams were turned into crude landing strips. Later, airports were built. The work on the airfields continued day and night in winter temperatures of -40 to -50° C and then in spring with impassable thawing roads. A variety of log houses were built for offices and living quarters. Land, frozen with permafrost, seemed to come to life as it was filled with the sounds of electric generators, airplane engines, cars, and heavy machinery. Airports were constructed in Yakutsk, Krasnoyarsk, and Kirensk. New airports were built in Uelkal and Markovo (Chukotka), and Seymchan on the Kolyma River. Alternate and intermediate airfields were built in Olyokminsk, Vitim, Tyoply Klyuch (Khandyga), Oymakon, Omolon, and Zyryanka.

Dictated by the necessities of the front, significant stress developed during the construction period. Basically, civilian workers performed the construction of the ALSIB airports located south of Yakutsk, while to the north and east of Yakutsk the trust *Dalstroy* (a powerful industrial company in the Northeastern territories of the country) conducted construction operations. During this time they scrounged convict labor — the hapless individuals from what are now known as the *Gulags* [Stalin's Labor Camps]. Additionally, the local population, primarily women, children, and the elderly, provided considerable help in the construction of the ALSIB airports. No fewer than 300 people worked daily on each airport.[7] As far as conditions permitted, the route was outfitted with radio equipment and weather stations. As the months passed, maps and aerial charts were made more precise along the route.

It is remarkable that in less than a year an air route of nearly five thousand kilometers was constructed. On August 11, 1942, the *Dalstroy* construction firm started work on an airport in Oymakon. By the end of September, a G-2 heavy 4-engine transport airplane landed there. On October 29th of the same year, the Aeroflot Commission put into service the Olyokminsk airport. The pre-war airport at Yakutsk was suitable only for servicing arriving and departing light airplanes, and, therefore, essentially had to be rebuilt.

Building equipment for construction of the airports, tanker trucks for gas and oil, and machine tools were delivered to the airports along the Arctic route and Lena River. Many offices and housing units

---

[6] I.S. Kychkin, "35 let nad polyusom kholoda," [35 years over the Pole of Cold], *Severnaya Trassa*, October 2, 1971, p. 3.

[7] *Natsionalny Arkhiv Respubliki Sacha (Yakutia),* [National Archives of Sacha Republic (Yakutia)], F. 52, Op. 33, D. 37, L. 19, 20.

were erected, including hangars for large cargo and military aircraft. In all, 26 airports and 274 wooden buildings were constructed and equipped along the airway under severe weather conditions.[8]

By the autumn of 1942, in just ten short months, on the huge territory between Uelkal in Chukotka and Krasnoyarsk, construction and reconstruction of 16 airports was completed. The Krasnoyarsk-Uelkal Air Route was officially put into service on January 30, 1943, by order of the head of the Chief Board of Civil Aviation.

In November of 1943, alternate airports in Nizhneilimsk (Irkutsk region), Vitim, Tyoply Klyuch (Khandyga) in Yakutia, and Anadyr in Chukotka were put into service. These alternate airports considerably increased flight safety along the route. As a result of the information gained during the first winter flights, a detour air route was opened along the warmer areas, bypassing Yakutsk and going instead through Uelkal, Magadan, and Kirensk.

The laying of a metal runway at Tanyurer in 1944. Courtesy of Ivan Negenblya.

The building of cargo-plane airports along the route continued until the close of the war. In Markovo, runways were paved with corrugated iron sheets made in the U.S. and delivered to the assembly location. By the end of 1944, airports in Tanyurer and Chaplino in Chukotka were put into service. To prepare for the war with Japan, construction of a 1,500 km air route from Yakutsk to the Far East was also built. Airports in Aldan underwent considerable reconstruction. Airports in Uchur and Tokko were constructed, and the 3,500 km route through Anadyr, Magadan, and Khabarobsk was put into service *[Figure 4, page 8 of this edition].*

The Route and Personnel

The Administration and Krasnoyarsk Air Route units that delivered aircraft from the U.S. to the Soviet Union began training in August 1942. The city of Ivanovo was selected for these units because it was located near the front line and had good airports and an Air Force training infrastructure already in place. Five Ferry Aviation Regiments [FARs] based in Fairbanks, Alaska, USA [1st FAR]; and in Uelkal [2nd FAR], Seymchan [3rd FAR], Yakutsk [4th FAR], and Kirensk [5th FAR], Soviet Union were formed.

---

[8] *Grazhdanskiy vozdushniy flot v Velikoy Otechestvennoy voine: stati, vospominaniya, dokumenty,* [The Civil Air Fleet in the Great Patriotic War: articles, memoirs, documents]. Moscow, 1985, p. 192.

Ground services were established, including aircraft repair and service shops, car pools, power supply, airport services, communication services, fuel and lubricants, and other services. Air bases in Uelkal, Markovo, Seymchan, Oymyakon, Yakutsk, Olyokminsk, and Kirensk were also constructed.[9] In all, about 3,000 people were projected to be employed on the route.

Pilots, engineers and technicians with war or arctic experience were selected. Some were recruited from the southern delivery route that ran from the port of Basra, via Iran, to Kirivobad, Azerbaijan. New personnel travelled to Ivanovo for orientation on flying foreign planes. Bomber squadrons underwent training flights at the Undol airport under the guidance of instructors from Lieutenant-Colonel P.I. Dmitriev's group. Fighter pilots were trained at the Ivanovo airport as well, but by Lieutenant-Colonel Shumov's flight team and Lieutenant-Colonel N.S. Vasin, Commander of the 1st Ferry Aviation Regiment.

Training included mastering the piloting technique of flying in closed cockpits, navigating long flights by compass, taking off and landing on short runways, and using radio navigation. With few exceptions, both pilots and radio operators had limited training in radio communication, and were completely unfamiliar with foreign radio equipment. Most of the trainees, including pilots and navigators, had no experience in the use of bearings, radio beacons, and non-directional beacons (NDBs) for navigation.[10]

While in flight, the gunner/radio operators were unable to maintain in-flight communication with any degree of confidence. They mainly received communications by air, but transmitted by key at a rate of only about 50-60 digital or letter signs per minute. International code was to be used on the route, but the radio operators were unfamiliar with it, and nobody could receive texts in mixed symbols.

The flights along the poorly equipped, insufficiently explored, and extremely long routes were impossible to cover by air without precisely organized radio communications with people capable of keeping up with important and uninterrupted communication during flights. Therefore, newly arriving personnel at Ivanovo, and regiments *en route*, had to learn to tune the receivers and transmitters to the required frequencies independently, to request bearings by microphone (especially fighter pilots) and to go out to the NDBs (Non-Directional Beacons) with the aid of a radio compass, under any weather conditions. Fighter pilots had to be able to go out to the NDB of the leading aircraft in case they lost contact with the wing. The navigators learned the detection method for the location of aircraft by two bearings.[11]

Navigator D.S. Sherl, a participant in those events from the very first days of the training flights, described how the U.S.S.R.'s airmen found themselves in difficult situations, because all the instructions and inscriptions in the aircraft and on the instrument panels were in English. Calculations were made in miles, feet, and gallons. Pilots and navigators drew translated tables on millimeter graph paper and glued them onto instrument panels of training aircraft. Quickly, however, the pilots learned the American measurement system and no longer needed the translated tables. As Sherl recollected, a far more difficult thing for U.S.S.R. pilots was to learn the flying capabilities of the foreign aircraft. Soviet pilots considered radio communication in fighter planes to be a novelty. Aircraft with a nose-wheel, instead of the more familiar tail-wheel, required special techniques for takeoff and landing.

Selection of pilots was very strict. After three unsuccessful attempts at taking off and landing, pilots were sent back to the Air Force's Personnel Department. Out of five newly arrived pilots, only one was accepted to the regiments being formed.[12]

On August 3, 1942, Colonel Ilya Pavlovich Mazuruk was appointed the commander of the 1st Ferry Aviation Division [FAD] and head of the Krasnoyarsk air route. The 1st FAD consisted of the

---

[9] *Prikaz Narodnogo Komissara Oborony SSSR No. 00162,* [The Order of the U.S.S.R. Peoples Defence Commissariat No. 00162], August 3, 1942.

[10] Radio navigation during this time used the ADF, Automatic Direction Finder, and the needle of this navigational aid always pointed to the Non-Directional Beacon or NDB.

[11] *Arkhiv Federalnoi sluzhby vozdushnogo transporta* (FSVT), [The Archives of the Soviet Federal Air Transport Service], F. 53, Op. 322, D. 39, L. 28.

[12] D.S. Sherl, "Aviamost: Alyaska-Sibir-front," [The Air Bridge: Alaska-Siberia-Front], *Na Severe Dalnem,* 1985, no. 1, p. 56.

Colonel Ilya Pavlovich Mazuruk, Commander of the 1st Ferry Aviation Division, 1942-1944. Courtesy of Ivan Negenblya.

five Ferry Aviation Regiments [FARs], each of which was responsible for its part of the route. The U.S.S.R.'s State Committee of Defense (SCD) believed that the selection of Colonel Mazuruk to this position would elevate the division's status in the eyes of the Allies. After all, Mazuruk was one of the first Heroes of the Soviet Union to earn a prestigious title for participation in Papanin's expedition to the North Pole in 1937. At the time, that event was widely publicized in the world press, so Mazuruk's name was somewhat familiar to the Americans. The commander had also led the Polar Aviation Department (*Glavsevmorput*), proving himself to be an outstanding organizer and leader of a large group of aviators. In addition to his fame as a polar pilot, the SCD believed that Mazuruk would be able to maintain notoriety among the Allies because he was a deputy of the Supreme Soviet—a rank equivalent to an American Congressman.

By September 1, 1942, the formation of the route and ferry regiments was complete. Staff and equipment were delivered from Ivanovo to Krasnoyarsk by rail and then by transport planes to permanent bases. To accelerate transportation, the 1st Ferry Aviation Regiment was flown by Li-2 planes [a Soviet-built copy of the Douglas DC-3] straight from Ivanovo to Ladd Field near Fairbanks, Alaska.

Yakutsk was chosen as the administrative center of the ferry route because the most powerful radio station in the northeast of the country and the Administration of Krasnoyarsk Air Route were there. Subsequently, the Ferry Division was housed in Yakutsk. The 4th Ferry Aviation Regiment and the 8th Transport Regiment were formed a little later in Yakutsk. The possibility of organizing aircraft maintenance in Yakutsk was also taken into consideration.

Soviet Mission to Alaska

The experts for the military mission in Alaska, headed by Lieutenant-Colonel M.G. Machin, were selected in haste. Those having experience with foreign equipment were recalled from Iraq and Iran. One of them, E.G. Radominov, a radio engineer, recalled:

> *Before departure to Alaska, about twenty engineers and technicians were invited to meet A.I. Mikoyan, who was in charge of supplying the army with food, fuel and uniforms. Anastas Ivanovich Mikoyan appeared to me as a simple man. He gave us farewell instructions approximately like this: 'You don't let us down abroad, especially don't get drunk. If you want to drink badly, do it where you live, lock yourselves in and hide your key. Nobody should see you drunk!'*
>
> *At the end of conversation Mikoyan asked: 'Well, and how about your uniforms? Is everything all right?'*

Our commissar, Lieutenant-Colonel, jumped up and reported:

— Comrade Narcom [People's Commissar], everything's all right we've been given the new uniforms!

And somebody of the technicians added:

— Yes, that's right, but they are made out of cotton, for the summer…

— Why so? — Mikoyan was surprised.

— There were not any other uniforms in the warehouse, — the commissar was trying to get out of the embarrassing situation.

Mikoyan picked up the phone and asked to connect him with Khrulyov, the Head of the Army's Quartermaster Corps, and said to him:

— Here is the group of experts going abroad. We have to provide them with good uniforms, custom made.

After that conversation we were sent at once to the Red Army tailor, where our measurements were taken. And in three days we were given uniform jackets and trousers of good quality.[13]

A few days after that meeting with Mikoyan, two Li-2 aircraft[14] with 50 experts on board left Moscow toward the East. Four additional planes from Ivanovo followed to Seymchan via Yakutsk, carrying 25 staff in each plane. There, on September 3, 1942, a man from Machin's group boarded an aircraft commanded by I.I. Moiseev and F.L. Ponomarenko. They took off and set course for Nome, Alaska. After a short stop at that first landing point on the American continent, they flew to Ladd Field, several kilometers outside of Fairbanks, Alaska. At Ladd Field, a meeting was held between the Soviet Embassy representatives and the American administrative delegation, hosted by the base commander, Brigadier General Dale V. Gaffney. They shared a modest but festive dinner party in the Officers' Club. All members of the Soviet military mission were invited.

At every encounter, the Americans showed hospitality and friendliness toward the Soviet aviators, and tensions were quickly eliminated. Employees of the Soviet mission had been coached before departure with instructive talks given by special state authorities. The delegation had been told: "Take caution, watch for possible provocations…" Surprisingly, in spite of the language barrier, the two groups communicated well, basically using facial expressions, gestures and exclamatory sounds, striking up animated, friendly "conversations" around the table.

American newspapers and magazine reporters of that time wrote that American and Soviet privates spent their free time together. "Some weeks ago, they took two boxes of beer, got on a jeep, and drove to the neighboring lake…" There were friendly relations between the officers as well. In February 1943, on Red Army day, the American officers were invited to the Soviets' quarters to celebrate the holiday. In response, in April, Soviet officers were invited to a dinner party in honor of the American Army. Some reporters noted that the Soviets liked American films and were fond of shopping and buying things in Fairbanks shops that were not available in wartime Soviet Union.

Reporters in the American press also wrote: "Both Americans and Russians, of course, learned some sentences and phrases in each other's language. But the Russians, even those who had very limited knowledge of English, could explain to the Americans what they wanted with help of language of gestures…Russians often say 'OK' and 'Okey dokey.' These expressions are often used in the American slang."[15]

The well thought-out location and layout of Ladd Field's buildings and services contrasted sharply with what the Soviets experienced at home. All airport services, barracks, apartments, canteen, club, and hangars were situated in a circle, connected by underground corridors. In winter, one could get to any location and service in light clothing through the well-heated tunnels, even in

---

[13] *Rukopis vospominaniy E.G. Radomirova* [E.G. Radominov's Memoir's Manuscript], Ivan Negenblya's, private collection.

[14] Li-2 is a licensed-built copy of the Douglas DC-3 transport plane; there are slight visual differences. [Editor].

[15] Ivan Negenblya, *Alyaska-Sibir: Trassa Muzhestva*. Yakutsk, 2000, pp. 85-86.

Colonel M.G. Machin, 1944. Courtesy of Ivan Negenblya.

temperatures of -40° C. Fighter planes were easily placed in spacious hangars. Nearby, large storage facilities were stocked with items necessary for the base operations, and for outfitting of the delivery route as well. Most striking for Soviet servicemen, who were used to a more "Spartan" life at small town Soviet Army bases, was the comfort of American military apartments in the far north. Personnel quarters were well cared for and of good design. Practical Americans explained to the Soviets that the expense for all that "luxury" was worth it.

The Soviet aviators in Alaska also lived in warm and spacious houses, unlike their colleagues in other ferry regiments located in remote U.S.S.R. territories. They ate at the garrison canteen, choosing from a variety of food, including fresh vegetables and fruit.

Training flights for the first group of Soviet airmen in Alaska were conducted by American instructors, Captain T. Harrel, Captain F. Cane and Lieutenant Nicholas de Tolli (great-grandson of Barklai de Tolli, the famous commander from the Napoleonic war of 1812). The 1st Regiment was made up of fighter pilots who had flown many battle hours in Soviet-made aircraft. In Alaska, however, they had to master American planes and, instead of combat flight, handle the less prestigious long-range delivery work. They were unaccustomed to ferrying planes; essentially, the Soviet pilots had to learn to fly again.

The language barrier presented a significant challenge in training. Only Lieutenant de Tolli was fluent in the Russian language. However, by using the language of gestures, and applying a lot of effort and good will, the Soviet pilots learned the rules and peculiarities of the American aircraft, and mastered the instructions from air traffic control.

It was also difficult for American instructors to accompany their Soviet apprentices in training flights. Only in B-25 bombers could instructors easily accompany the Soviet pilot trainees. In the A-20 aircraft, instructors barely fit into the seats behind the Soviets.[16] On one-seat fighter planes, there was no seat for an instructor at all, so the Soviet pilots had to depend on oral instructions from the ground. Once in the air, the Russian-speaking apprentice pilot was virtually alone and could rely only on himself. Despite the difficulties, the first group of Soviet pilots completed their training in just five days.

Colonel Machin, head of the U.S.S.R. mission in the U.S.A. from 1942 to 1944, noted that relations with American servicemen and citizens in Fairbanks and Nome were good and friendly. He often cited one remarkable fact: it was not only in the Soviet Union that factories, collective farm workers, and individual working people bought tanks, planes, and other battle equipment from their savings. Schoolgirls from Buffalo, N.Y. (where the Bell aviation factory was located) also bought a fighter-plane with money they had collected, and presented it to the Soviet airmen. One of the 1st Ferrying Aviation Regiment's best pilots, V.I. Suvorov, took off from the airport in Fairbanks in this plane, but, unfortunately the fate of this plane is unknown.

The Soviets learned to trust General Gaffney and found him to be a man of his word who fulfilled his Allied duties with honesty, and was extremely helpful to the Soviet mission. This was demonstrated in December 1942, when the weather in the arctic was so cold that hydraulic fluid

---

[16] The A-20 was a single-pilot airplane with no second seat for a co-pilot, but it was possible to lie prone behind the pilot in a space beneath the upper hatch and look over the pilot's shoulder. [Editor].

thickened, destroying hydraulic lines in the American aircraft. About one hundred battle aircraft waited helplessly in the Chukotka and Yakutia airfields. Machin reported the problem to General Gaffney who immediately contacted scientists at the University of Alaska Fairbanks, representatives of aviation firms, and others. On Gaffney's request, in just two days chemists found a hydraulic fluid additive resistant to freezing, and aircraft manufacturing firms supplied frost-resistant rubber hoses. Just as efficiently, in only a few days, portable heaters with two or three hoses for supplying hot air to aircraft systems became available at Ladd Field. These heaters were immediately flown to the frozen battle planes in Chukotka and Yakutia via C-47 transport planes.

About the same time, cases of scurvy began to appear at Chukotka due to a lack of sufficient quantities of vegetables for the military garrisons. With the long winter ahead, and the threat of an epidemic a grave concern, Colonel Machin asked the Americans for help. Gaffney set up agreements with trading companies and within several days all the necessary vegetables and scurvy medicines had been delivered by air to the garrisons in the U.S.S.R.

Help among Americans, Soviet specialists, and business persons was mutual. Friendly relations were established and they consulted each other on various problems. American experts highly valued the abilities of the Soviet pilots, engineers, and technicians. Once, for example, a Soviet engineer was invited during the winter to Edmonton, Canada, to help solve a complicated technical problem affecting 60 aircraft standing idle on the ground. As a result of joint efforts, in a short time the cause of the problem was located and addressed, and the planes delivered to their assigned destination.

Left to right: E.A. Makarova, translator; G.T. Smirnov, engineer; American engineer; and N.P. Borovikov, engineer. Fairbanks, Alaska 1943. Courtesy of Ivan Negenblya.

Two Soviet translators, Yelena A. Makarova and Nina Fenelonova, both of whom had graduated from the Military Department of the Moscow Institute of Foreign Languages, translated technical texts and other documents received by the Soviet mission in Fairbanks. Almost none of the engineers, technicians, and pilots knew English, so the women would interpret at presentations given by American manufacturers. When Soviet men were hospitalized, Makarova and Fenelonova dropped in to visit the patients before work. Patients and doctors alike impatiently awaited their arrival each day so they could interpret. Thus, Makarova and Fenelonova had the difficult task of mastering not only technical translations, but medical terminology as well.

Interpreting the movies at the Officers' Club proved an uncomfortable duty for the women. Soviet officers were allotted two rows in the hall. The women would quickly translate the dialog into Russian for those next to them who would then pass the information on to their neighbors. That, of course, disturbed the American viewers, but they treated the inconvenience with understanding.[17]

---

[17] *Rukopis vospominaniy Ye.A. Makarovoy*, [Yelena A. Makarova's Memoirs], Ivan Negenblya's private collection.

At times, misunderstandings arose between the Soviet and American missions in Alaska. In the summer of 1943, an American driver who had been working at the air base mysteriously disappeared. It was later learned that he had drowned in a lake. There was suspicion that the Soviet representatives were somehow involved in the incident. The air base command ordered that every pilot carry photo identification and that aircraft be searched before departure. Machin forbade the search, but after that Soviet pilots could not depart Ladd Field without special permission. After Machin went to General Gaffney, a new, more scrupulous investigation of the circumstances of the driver's death was conducted. Eventually, everything was cleared up, and relations between the Allies improved again.

Engineer E.G. Radominov described details of aircraft receiving and transferring in Fairbanks, and the circumstances surrounding Soviet engineer V.B. Kiselnikov's death:

The established process of transferring of the aircraft was as follows: at first our experts inspected the aircraft on the ground, made a list of their imperfections, translated them into English and handed it over to the Americans. They repaired the detected defects and if there were no problems on the next inspection, the act of transfer was signed and then the aircraft was test-flown.

I received the radio equipment of the aircraft being transferred. The equipment of the fighters and A-20 bombers I tested on the ground, equipment on B-25 bombers and C-47 transport aircraft on the ground and then in the air. The fighters and A-20 bombers were test-flown by our pilots and sometimes they flew the B-25s and C-47s together with the Americans — a pilot and a flight mechanic. In that case I checked the radio equipment in the air, and Kiselnikov tested the aircraft and engine systems and the instruments.

Soviet and American pilots at Ladd Field, Fairbanks, 1944. Courtesy of Ivan Negenblya.

In December 1942 the Americans brought B-25s. The American crew, Kiselnikov and I were to test-fly the plane. Not long before that, Machin gave an order: not to fly without parachutes. All of us were given personal parachutes, which were stored in the separate room in the hangar, and the armament engineer gave them out.

That test flight was planned for after dinnertime, and the darkness set in after 2:00 pm Kiselnikov and I came for parachutes but the engineer was absent—he had left the hangar. Kiselnikov found Machin's personal parachute under the table in our room and said he would fly with it. I didn't find a parachute and being a disciplined man I had to refuse to fly and asked Kiselnikov to check the radio communication in flight. He agreed.

At about 1:00 pm they took off and at the end of the airport they lost altitude and crashed from the height of 100 meters. All of them died. I was lucky.[18]

The Aircraft over the Tundra and *Taiga*

Bombers and transport airplanes were usually flown one at a time or in groups of two or three. Fighters, as a rule, were flown in wedge-shaped groups, headed by a bomber leader close ahead. A bomber or fighter squadron leader would bring up the rear.

Because the fighters had a limited range, the entire 6,575-kilometer [4,086 miles] route from Fairbanks to Krasnoyarsk was divided into five stages. Each stage had its own Ferry Aviation Regiment that operated only within its own stage. After passing the planes to their destination at the neighboring regiment, the pilots returned to their base by transport aircraft flown by a special squadron, the 8th Transport Aviation Detachment, formed on July 4, 1943, and commanded by Lieutenant-Colonel V.A. Pushchinsky.

The delivery of the aircraft was performed as follows: American pilots ferried the airplanes from aircraft factories in the U.S., across Canada, to Fairbanks, where the Soviet Military Mission representatives received them. In Fairbanks, the planes were taken by the 1st FAR pilots (commanded by Lieutenant-Colonel P. Nedosekin, and later Lieutenant-Colonel N.S. Vasin), and flown to Nome, Alaska, and then across the Bering Strait to Uelkal, the airport on the coast of the Anadyrsky Gulf, Chukotka. This stage of the route was 1,560 kilometers long [970 miles]. These flights were hindered by prolonged and constant fog from the sea, thunderstorms over Alaska, and severe winter frosts and snowstorms. On the Bering Strait crossing to the Uelkal stage, there were fewer flying days a year than in any stage along the whole route. Because of Alaska's extreme weather conditions, during 1944 on the Fairbanks-Nome stage there were only 109 flying days, compared to 181 flying days on the Yakutsk-Kirensk stage.

The 2nd Ferry Aviation Regiment, commanded by Lieutenant-Colonel A.G. Melnikov and later Lieutenant-Colonel M.I. Pavlenkov, was stationed in Uelkal. The 2nd FAR was responsible for aircraft delivery via the most difficult 1,450-km [902 miles] stage from Uelkal over the uninhabited Chukotka, the Kolymsky Ridge, and on to Seymchan.

The 3rd stage, 1,200 km [745 miles] from Seymchan to Yakutsk, was also not easy; it went over the Chersky and Verkhoyansk Ridges through the Oymyokon region. Quite often pilots had to fly at high altitude at very low temperatures, wearing oxygen masks. From Seymchan, aviators from the 3rd Ferry Aviation Regiment, commanded by Lieutenant-Colonel N. Tverdokhlebov and later by Major V.I. Frolov, piloted the airplanes to Oymyokon, Khandyga and then to Yakutsk. Oymyokon earned its nickname, the "Pole of Cold." In the winter of 1944, temperatures registered at -50°C on 69 days. In Yakutsk, 21 days dipped to that same low temperature.[19] Thick fogs accompanied the heavy frosts. Therefore, from the 2nd half of November until mid February, the delivery of aircraft was carried out mainly along the Okhotsky seacoast route, via Magadan to Kirensk, and then onto the main route.

---

[18] *Rukopis vospominaniy E.G. Radominova*, [E.G. Radominov's Memoir's Manuscript], Ivan Negenblya's, private collection.

[19] *The Report of the 1st Red Banner Ferrying Air Division in 1944*, p. 19, Ivan Negenblya's private collection.

V.M. Perov in the cockpit. Courtesy of Ivan Negenblya.

Technical difficulties hindered takeoff from Yakutsk. Here, the maintenance personnel's job was even more difficult than in Uelkal. That year, winter had set in early, and the temperatures had dropped to -50°C. Many people suffered from frostbite. Aircraft not adapted for those conditions had many technical problems. There were those who wondered, "Is it at all possible to fly 'the tender Americans' in our Far North conditions?" But engineers and technicians asserted their self-control, quick wits, and willpower. All weak points that required more careful warming were found, and this was done before each flight.

At last, in the cold morning of November 4, 1942, fighters, led by Lieutenant-Colonel V.V. Fokin, the Deputy Chief of Krasnoyarsk Air Route, in an A-20 bomber, headed for Kirensk, where they arrived in 5 ½ hours. It was not done without difficulties. The cold was bitter. When they approached Kirensk, the fluid in their hydraulic systems got so thick that the landing gear in the aircraft lowered only with great difficulty, in emergency mode.

Again, they had to wait for good weather. And when there was no improvement, they had to deliver the aircraft to Krasnoyarsk anyway. On November 11, 1942, Fokin gave an order to depart. That was a very risky flight. Much of the time they flew quite low, and had to face low clouds and snow. As they approached Krasnoyarsk, the weather got better. The planes landed at the airport and were received by representatives from the Air Force Commandant's office. At once, the aircraft were sent to the Stalingrad front by railway. The delivery of this first group of fighters had taken more than a month.[24]

By the beginning of the winter campaign of November 19, 1942, through 1943, 211 foreign manufactured fighters and 116 bombers were on the frontline of the Soviet Air Force along the Soviet-German front.[25] They didn't have much influence on the balance of opposing troops in the beginning, but they served as a morale booster; the Soviets then knew that they were not alone in their fight with the enemy. Thus, the ferry convoy on the Alaska-Siberia (ALSIB) route was launched, and the Air Bridge ALSIB began to operate.

In October of 1942, the Soviets received the first four C-47 aircraft in Fairbanks. Each crew consisted of two pilots, a flight mechanic, and a radio operator. Sometimes they flew without a co-pilot. After learning the performance of the aircraft and unfamiliar instrument readings in inches, feet, and miles, and after two training flights with the American instructor Nicholas de Tolli, the crew received the aircraft. Captain G.S. Benkunsky, who was in that first group, recollected:

The absence of a navigator in the crew made the orientation difficult, especially with quite inaccurate charts. Besides, the flights were done at high altitudes, as a rule, in clouds or above them. Quite often we had to fly the planes at night, which is why VFR [Visual Flight Rules] was practically excluded. True, we had had sufficient experience in night flights, because at the front we flew without navigators as well, and we performed the flights deep into the enemy territory. The principal orientation method on route was radio bearings from the ground direction finders. In that condition the radio operator's role increased considerably, as it was practically impossible to fly without him.[26]

[24] V.M. Perov, "V nachale peregonki," [At the Beginning of Ferry], *Trassa muzhestra i druzhby*. Yakutsk: The National Publishing House of the Sacha Republic (Yakutia), 1992, pp. 192, 193.

[25] I.P. Lebedev, *Kobry letyat k frontu*. [The Cobras Fly to the Frontline]. Moscow: Voenizdat, 1992, p. 70.

[26] G.S. Benkunsky, "Perezhitoye Zanovo," [Outliving Anew], *Grazhdanskaya Aviatsiya* [Civil Aviation], 1990, no. 11, p. 18.

Stalingrad Story

Your children's children will thrill to the story of Stalingrad.

—of the besieged, battered, hopeless city that was saved by white hooded infantrymen crawling on their bellies in swirling wastes of snow.

—saved by heroic ground forces whose magnificent air support never failed them.

Bell Airacobras, roaring over the Stalingrad front, gave wings to artillery. Above the masses of men and tanks locked in combat on the ground, they hunted out the enemy's vital spots—blasted them at short range with explosive and armor piercing cannon shells. Providing air support for ground troops is a job the Airacobra does superlatively well.

Here's the significant point. Airacobras were there in force when they were needed. We're able to deliver planes for action now *when they're needed* in this global war, because we started early enough, planned well enough and pushed production hard enough.

After victory we'll be telling you about new Bell planes, planes of peace. What will they be like? Well, they'll be designed, engineered and built by an organization that makes a habit of aviation pioneering. © Bell Aircraft Corporation, Buffalo and Niagara Falls, New York.

Airacobras for victory —
FUTURE PLANES FOR PEACE
BELL *Aircraft*
PACEMAKER OF AVIATION PROGRESS

From the back cover of the August 1943 issue of Bellringer *magazine, a publication of the Bell Aircraft Company in Buffalo, NY. 2,618 Bell P-39 Airacobras and 2,397 Bell P-63 Kingcobras were ferried from Buffalo, New York via Montana and Alaska to the Russian battlefronts. Courtesy of the Niagara Aerospace Museum collection, Niagara Falls, NY.*

The pilots and crew of the transport planes on the ferry route were considered auxiliary, yet their work was very demanding and required a great deal of responsibility. Delivery of the military aircraft, and the operation as a whole, depended upon their work. After delivering fighter planes and bombers to pilots at the next stage, the ferry pilots returned to their regiment's airports as passengers on C-47 transport aircraft so that they could fly the next Lend-Lease plane to the next pick-up point. In addition to flying these pilots, the transport crew carried large amounts of cargo. The C-47 pilots and crew flew twice as frequently as the pilots ferrying the Lend-Lease planes. Twenty or more experienced flyers piloted these transports along the route.

Engineering and technical staff held demanding jobs as well. A.S. Tkachenko, who worked as a technician for special equipment in the 4th FAR throughout the entire Lend-Lease operation, recollected:

> *If the weather allowed, arrivals and departures were accomplished every day. When we let out the crew of the 4th Regiment in Kirensk, immediately the 3rd Regiment's crew arrived from Seymchan. As a rule, there were a lot of aircraft. We serviced them, fixed any defects, and removed batteries for recharging and storage. Before you noticed, it was night time. Then at 4 a.m. we had to be at the workplace to prepare the planes for departure. Failures of altimeters were a frequent problem. Replacing those instruments on the "Airacobra" took a lot of work because the gun had to be removed first. After repairing tachometers and testing level gauges, we started up the engines. Heating them was accomplished by wood burning stoves. We moved heavy items like batteries, with the help of one horse.[27]*

Airplanes at Uelkal airfield waiting for flying weather conditions. Courtesy of Ivan Negenblya.

---

[27] A.S. Tkachenko, "Polyot nachinaetsya na zemle" [The Flight Begins on the Land], *Trassa muzhestva i druzhby*. Yakutsk: Sacha Republic, pp. 185, 186.

For the three months from October through December of 1942, 114 airplanes were delivered to the Soviet territory from Fairbanks. These included 54 A-20 bombers, 8 B-25 bombers, 41 P-40 fighters, and 11 P-39 fighters. Among these, 31 airplanes (6 A-20 bombers, 6 B-25 bombers, and 19 P-40 fighters) were delivered to Krasnoyarsk along the Alaska-Siberia Air Route.[28] Soviet aviators delivered that small number of aircraft at great expense, with 31 losing their lives in crashes. This high fatality rate occurred because the flying and engineering staff had insufficient training and lacked experience operating aircraft in Siberia's brutal winters and under such severe weather conditions.

For the first time ever, the division and regiment command had to plan for special conditions as they organized these mass flights of military and transport planes in the northern latitudes. During the winter months, the duration of daylight was often equal to or shorter than the duration of a flight leg. For example, the Uelkal to Seymchan leg of the route could be flown in 4 hours 20 minutes at a speed of 200 miles per hour. The duration of daylight was only 4 hours 40 minutes. If the weather deteriorated in the middle of the flight, and the intermediate airport was closed, the crew could not return to the departure airport.

There was no time to detour around bad weather areas. Landing airports, especially in the eastern section of the route, were exposed to unexpected abrupt changes in weather. Pilots were unable to receive actual weather reports along the route, since the shortage of daylight impeded accurate researching of weather conditions. By the time the weather researcher could get to the landing station, darkness had set in at the departure airport. Therefore, the C-47 transport airplane was often sent ahead of the Lend-Lease planes in the dark, to investigate night-time weather conditions.

It was the Regiment Commander's important duty to collect weather data along the whole route before making the decision to allow dozens of aircraft to depart. This became the principal task for the Commander and his staff. I.P. Mazuruk's recollections provide insight into some of the difficulties endured by the ferry aviators:

> *In February 1943 a group of 12 Airacobras, led by myself, had to land on the frozen Kolyma River, near the village of Zyryamka, because the destination airport of Seymchan was closed due to thick fog. In Zyryanka the thermometer showed -46° C. There were no heaters. But the next morning the entire group of airplanes took off. That flight was possible, thanks to the leader-bomber's (B-25) mechanic Dmitry Ostrovenko who called for help from local inhabitants. All night long the people of Zyryanka, under his supervision, stoked iron stoves set under the Airacobras covered with large pieces of tarpaulin.[29]*

Some emergency landings and crashes, fortunately, ended without fatality. On December 9, 1942, on the Seymchan to Yakutsk route over the Verkhoyansk Range, and in severe cold, oil started leaking from the engine on a P-40 aircraft flown by the 3rd FAR pilot, Junior Lieutenant M.A. Dyakov. The pilot made an emergency belly landing on the river near the Verkhoyansk Mountains. The group's leader, in the aircraft bringing up the rear, didn't keep track of Dyakov's fix so he didn't know the exact point of his landing. As a result, several days of intensified air searches for the pilot were carried out unsuccessfully. Later, after the river thawed, the plane sunk. The pilot, on the other hand, was found and brought to safety by a specially equipped dog sled expeditionary team.

On June 17, 1943, Major V.I. Polyansky, the 3rd FAR Commander, was flying a P-39 fighter from Markovo to Seymchan. After an hour and a half in the air he noticed an engine vibration. Manipulations undertaken by the pilot didn't improve the situation. The engine kept misfiring, while the coolant temperature reached its maximum. The oil pressure fell below an acceptable level, and a burning

---

[28] *Arkhiv Federalnoy sluzhby vozdushnogo transporta* (FSVT), [The Archives of the Russian Federal Air Transport Service], F. 44-C, Op. 2, D. 134, L. 6, p.t.o. 7.

[29] A.A. Lebedev and I.P. Mazuruk, *Nad Arktikoy i Antarcktikoy*, [Over the Arctic and Antarctic]. Moscow: Mysl, 1991, p. 54.

smell permeated the cabin. To prevent the engine's breakdown and fire in the air, Polyansky made a belly landing into the soggy summer marshes of the region, at the mouth of the Levy Kedon River. The landing was successful, with only some bending of the propeller blades and a small dent on the right control surface. Upon inspection, the pilot found only two liters of oil remaining in the engine, and no coolant at all. The uninjured pilot was taken to the airport. Some months later, when the ground froze in winter, they managed to evacuate the aircraft from its forced landing location.

During the war people not only died on the front lines, but also far from the battlefields. During the operation of the Alaska-Siberia Airway, on the Soviet side alone there were 44 crashes in which 113 Soviet aviators perished. Today, at the sites of these accidents and burials can be found unpretentious monuments, tombstones, and obelisks.

The Reorganization and Enhanced Efficiency of the Route

From the beginning of the route, I.P. Mazuruk acted as both the division commander and the head of the Krasnoyarsk Air Route. During the first year, it became evident that one person was unable to deal properly with such a large variety of difficult issues and problems. Subsequently, after June 15, 1943, the Krasnoyarsk to Uelkal Air Route Administration was established, with all airports in this route falling under this command. Major General I.S. Semyenov headed the Administration initially; after August of 1944, Lieutenant General M.I. Shevelyev took over. Ferry and Transport Regiments became an independent entity, and the 1st Ferry Aviation Division was commanded by Colonel I.P. Mazuruk until May of 1944, when command was turned over to Colonel A.G. Melnikov.

During 1943, the Soviet Union's Aviation Industry turned out 35,000 military aircraft. In the same period of time, along the Alaska-Siberia route, 2,465 aircraft were delivered to the Soviet territory. Among them were 186 B-25 bombers, 771 A-20 fighters, 6 P-40s, 1,343 P-39s, 3 P-47s, and 156 C-47 transport airplanes.[30] Thanks to these extraordinary efforts, by January 1, 1944, for the first time during the war, the Red Army's Air Force aviation units and military training schools were provided, in full, with proper aircraft.

The heroic labor of the ferry aviators and personnel on the Alaska-Siberia route was greatly appreciated by the Supreme Command and recognized by Decree of the Presidium of the U.S.S.R. Supreme Soviet. In February of 1944, the 1st Ferry Aviation Division was awarded the Red Banner order for exemplary fulfillment of the tasks set by the Command for ferrying the military aircraft. The Division was renamed the 1st Red Banner Ferry Aviation Division. As a result of this recognition, 551 members of the division were honored with combat orders and medals.[31]

Organization and management of delivery in 1944-45 was changed completely. In the previous period, when all the detachments were operating independently, aircraft were flown only in "their" section, with detachment commanders in charge of their ferry detachments only. After 1944, however, there was continual movement of the ferry detachments throughout the route in order to increase efficiency and the rate of aircraft ferrying.

The reorganization was very successful. During February and March of 1944, the division delivered 1,010 planes to Krasnoyarsk, 573 of them in March alone—the largest number of planes shipped along the route during one month for the tenure of the entire operation. This exceeded the delivery plan for a month, as set by the State Committee of Defense, by 250%.[32] During 1944, 3,418 planes were delivered along the route. In comparison to the previous year, the airplane delivery at the destination point increased by 80%, fulfilling the delivery plan set by the government in 1944 by 114%. The maximum number of the airplanes delivered in a day in 1944 was 88, compared to 57 in 1943. Additionally, flight accidents were cut in half, and irretrievable losses reduced two and a half times.[33]

---

[30] *Arkhiv Federalnoy sluzhby vozdushnogo transporta* (FSVT), [The Archives of the Russian Federal Air Transport Service], F. 44-C, Op. 2, D. 134, L. 6, 7.

[31] Ibid., D. 196, L. 25.

[32] Ibid., L. 4.

[33] Ibid., F. 44-C, Op. 2, D. 139, L. 12.

Lend-Lease aircraft over Kamchatka Peninsula. Courtesy of Ivan Negenblya.

The Sunset of the ALSIB Airway

By spring of 1945, the Allies were fully confident of a victory over Nazi Germany, and the Soviet Union started preparations for the war campaign in the Far East against Japan. In March of 1945, the 1st Ferry Aviation Division administration flew a C-47 over the route planned for ferrying American airplanes to the Far East and Trans-Baykal fronts, and also for the Pacific Navy. The administrators detailed all of the issues necessary for consideration to safely and securely deliver the planes, and, after this flight, the Division Headquarters developed specific instructions for regiments concerning delivery conditions, navigators' services, communications, and weather information.

After the victory over Germany, the delivery of American fighters and bombers to the Soviet Union continued for four more months; these concentrated on the airports in Markovo, Yakutsk, and Krasnoyarsk. Several hundred airplanes accumulated at the Krasnoyarsk airport. After June 26, 1945, aircraft delivery commenced from Yakutsk to Ukurey, Kuybyshevka, and Vladivostok. In July, the route was started from Markovo to Elizovo (Kamchatka). Intensive aircraft delivery from Yakutsk, Markovo, and Krasnoyarsk to Petropavlovsk-Kamchatsky, Ukurey, Chita, Khabarovsk, the 111th siding track, and Vladivostok continued in August and September. The planes flown through these locations at this time went to the Air Forces of the Far East and Trans-Baykal fronts, as well as to the Pacific Ocean Navy.[34]

By August 9, 1945, three Air Force Armies in the Far East and Trans-Baykal were at war with Japan, and 6.9% of their total warplanes were Lend-Lease aircraft.[35] Also in the war with Japan, a squadron of seven crews of C-47 aircraft from the 8th Transport Aviation Regiment (a detachment from the 9th Air Army of the first Far East front) took part in the landing operation at the rear of the *Kwantung* Army. This squadron supplied the airports of Kharbin, Girin, and Chanchun with fuel and ammunition for the troops operating in the region of Mudandzyan. The 30 person staff of the squadron was given

---

[34]   Ibid., Sheet 14.

[35]   I.P. Lebedev, *Kobry letyat k frontu*. [The Cobras Fly to the Frontline]. Moscow: Voenizdat, 1992, p. 71.

state awards.[36] Also, for the exemplary fulfillment of their duties and successful delivery of aircraft, aviation units in the Fair East front, including the 152 members of the 1st Ferry Aviation Division, were rewarded with the medal "For the Victory over Japan." Several months earlier, personnel taking part in delivering the Lend-Lease aircraft had been awarded the medals "For the Victory over Germany."

At the end of August 1945, the delivery of Lend-Lease aircraft to the Soviet Union ended, as the United States stopped delivery. Disassembly of ferry route structures began. The 1st FAR was transferred from Fairbanks to Markovo, from which military aircraft were moved to Petropavlovsk-Kamchatsky, and also to Vladivostok. The planes went to the aviation divisions involved in the war with Japan. In October, the 1st FAR was disbanded and its staff sent to the Red Army Air Force units. Only the 8th Transport Regiment of the 1st FAR was transferred under authority of the head of the Krasnoyarsk-Uelkal Air Route and given to Civil Aviation.[37] On January 11, 1945, 127 personnel (among them 29 captains of the aircraft, 21 co-pilots and 36 flight technicians) were attached to the 8th Transport Regiment.

In a November 16, 1945 order, the U.S.S.R.'s Internal Trade Commissar, A.I. Mikoyan, summed up the final result of the Soviet aviators' work in Alaska :

On the Liquidation of the Air Base in Fairbanks

1. *To consider that the Soviet air base in Fairbanks (Alaska, U.S.A.) is closed as of October 24, 1945 and the work of operative group for liquidation of the base is completed.*

2. *To thank officially the whole personnel of the air base for perfect fulfillment of the tasks put before the air base staff and for excellent organization of technical services on receiving of foreign military and transport aircraft from the Americans and preparing them for transfer to the U.S.S.R.[38]*

In early 1946, the Alaska-Siberia Ferrying Route ceased all activities. Many people who served on the ALSIB route had taken a liking to the northern region, and, after demobilization, stayed in Yakutia to form the backbone of the Yakut Civil Aviation. Some of the specialists of the 8th Transport and Ferry Regiment and of other subdivisions of the route joined the staff of the East Siberian, Far East and other administrations of U.S.S.R. Civil Aviation. Many with experience on the route stayed and staffed the Yakut Republic Aviation detachments and airports. In some families of ferrying pilots who had settled in Yakutia, the aviation profession has continued on from generation to generation.

The ALSIB Contribution to Victory in WWII

How many aircraft were delivered along the Alaska-Siberia route? Unfortunately, different data are cited by various sources. The most reliable source may be the one, divided into the years and types of the delivered planes, as presented by "The Service List of the 1st Red Banner Ferry Aviation Division." The List states that between October 1942 and October 1945, 8,094 airplanes were transported via Alaska and handed over to the U.S.S.R. Among the types included were P-40 - 43, A-20 - 1,330, B-25 - 725, P-39 - 2,593, C-47 - 705, P-47 - 3, P-63 - 2,640, C-46 - 1, and At-6 - 54.[39]

In all, the U.S.S.R. obtained from the Allies 22,195 airplanes via various routes—nearly 10% of the total number of aircraft that took part in the war on the Soviet side.[40] Of the fighter planes, about 19%

---

[36] *Arkhiv Federalnoi sluzhby vozdushnogo transporta* (FSVT), [The Archives of the Russian Federal Air Transport Service], F. 44-C, Op. 2, D. 139, L. 14.

[37] The Order of Civil Aviation Head Office No. 0243, October 20, 1945.

[38] The copy of the order is in Negenblya's private collection.

[39] *Arkhiv Federalnoi sluzhby vozdushnogo transporta* (FSVT), [The Archives of the Russian Federal Air Transport Service], F. 44-C, Op. 2, D. 139, L. 15.

[40] V.N. Chernavin, "Lend-Lease v sisteme Vtoroy Mirovoy Voiny," [Lend-Lease in World War II System], *Mir Istorii*, 2000, no. 2; //http:www.fellar.ru/historia/archive/02-001chernavin.htm.

were Lend-Lease aircraft, with 1 in 5 fighters being American or English.[41] Many Air Force and Naval Aviation regiments of the Soviet Union were supplied totally by the Allies' airplanes. A squadron commanded by A.I. Pokryshkin (three-time Hero of the Soviet Union) flew P-39 Airacobra and P-63 Kingcobra fighters from the beginning of 1943 to the end of the war. Pokryshkin's squadron pilots, who were particularly noted for their skill and courage, brought fame to themselves and to their American aircraft. [42]

In a July 11, 1945 message from the Chairman of the Council of Ministers of the U.S.S.R., Joseph Stalin, to U.S. President Harry Truman, the Soviet leader assessed the Lend-Lease deliveries, recognizing "…they played an important role and assisted in the successful completion of the war against our common enemy, Nazi Germany, to a great extent."[43]

ALSIB on the Diplomatic Service

International airlines linking the Soviet Union with foreign countries ceased operation after the war broke out, with active flights continuing only between Moscow and Tehran. In March of 1942, the British Air Mission in Moscow applied to the Soviet government for establishment of air service between Great Britain and the U.S.S.R., to begin in the spring and summer of the same year. In negotiations it was agreed that re-equipped transport versions of "Albimal-1" bombers would fly that route. The first flights on the route, however, turned out to be dangerous, since they flew over war operations. Additionally, the aircraft themselves proved unreliable. By the middle of 1943 they had to give up on that project.[44]

When the Alaska-Siberia route began operating regularly, thanks to the selfless and well-coordinated operation of the pilots, engineers and technicians, and gained a good reputation for being one of the world's most reliable routes, it began to be used for other international travels. Andrei Gromyko, who had been the U.S.S.R. Ambassador to the U.S. since August 1943, recognized that fact when he said:

The reliable route from Moscow to Washington DC was the only route which passed through all our country: via Siberia, the Far East to Alaska, and then abruptly to the South to Canada and from there to the American capital.[45]

The Krasnoyarsk-Yakutsk-Fairbanks route was often used to fly diplomats and statesmen to and from both countries. Besides Gromyko, the Soviet Foreign Commissar V.M. Molotov and prominent Soviet diplomats K.A. Umansky and M.M. Litvinov also flew the route. In the spring of 1944, while traveling to China and the Soviet Union, the Vice-President of the U.S., Henry Wallace,[46] and U.S. Senator W. Wilkey used the ALSIB route.[47]

The route was also used when delegations from the U.S.S.R., Great Britain, and China traveled to a conference in the U.S. on the issue of universal security to discuss agreements later adopted in the conference in Moscow in October 1943. At this meeting, proposals were developed to establish the international security organization that laid down the foundations of the United Nations. As a result,

---

[41] V.P. Kotelnikov, "Aviatsionny Lend-Lease," [The Lend-Lease Aviation], *Voprosy Istorii*, 1991, no. 9-10, pp. 223-227.

[42] *Samolyotostroenie v SSSR: 1917-1945*, [The Aircraft Building in the U.S.S.R.: 1917-1945], volume 2. Moscow: TSAGI, 1994, pp. 250, 251.

[43] *The Soviet-American Relations during the Great Patriotic War 1941-1945: Documents and Materials*. Moscow, 1984, vol. 2, p. 437.

[44] *Po stranam i kontinentam*, [Around Countries and Continents]. Moscow: Federal Aviation Service RF, 1998, pp. 27-29.

[45] A.A. Gromyko, *Pamyatnoye*, [The Memorable], volume 1. Moscow: Politizdat, 1990, p. 164.

[46] *Po stranam i kontinentam*, [Around Countries and Continents]. Moscow: Federal Aviation Service RF, 1998, p. 31.

[47] A. Chuba and D. Sherl, "Trassa Mazuruka," [Mazuruk's Route], *Sovetskaya Rossiya*, 1986, no. 163, p. 2.

G.S. Benkunsky, C-47 Commander. Courtesy of Ivan Negenblya.

the crew of the 8th Transport Regiment serviced many international flights.[48]

By the beginning of the war, the Soviet aviation industry had achieved success in building military aircraft. However, no multi-seated passenger planes had yet been constructed. As yet, the U.S.S.R. had no comfortable aircraft in which they could fly delegations of State. Therefore, in May-June 1942, V.M. Molotov, the second in command in the Soviet State, paid a crucial visit to Great Britain and the U.S., traveling aboard the most powerful Soviet bomber, the Pe-8.

Later, a C-47 of the 8th Transport Regiment was used to bring the Soviet delegation to the U.S. The crew consisted of G.S. Benkunsky, Captain; M. Maksimenko, co-pilot; P.N. Borisov, flight mechanic; and V.D. Glazkov, radio operator. In the morning of August 3, 1942, Benkunsky's aircraft took off from the Yakutsk airport. By noon of the next day it landed in Vnukovo, Moscow. From there, the aircraft was urgently sent to a maintenance base. Within a week, it was re-equipped beyond recognition. The cargo compartment was transformed into a comfortable cabin with ten soft seats along the left side, and a table with two armchairs on the right. In the area between the cockpit and the cabin, where additional fuel tanks had been located, two beds were installed. The ceiling and side panels down to the windows were covered with blue velvet, and below to the floor with light-brown leather-like vinyl. The floor was covered in carpet.

In the morning of August 12, 1942, the Soviet delegation, headed by A.A. Gromyko, then U.S.S.R. Consul to the U.S., left Moscow. After a short stop in Sverdlovsk, the aircraft arrived in Krasnoyarsk where the passengers and crew stayed the night. Early the next morning, they were airborne again. Under the airplane's wings lay the dense *taiga*. Rivers gleamed in the sun from time to time. After nine hours of flight, the plane flew over the Lena River, then landed in Yakutsk. That night, the delegation was accommodated in what was considered at the time a splendid new airport hotel.

The next day, on August 15, they were again airborne. Against the background of dark-green *taiga* the ribbon-like Aldan River wound its way along the foothills of the Verkhoyansk Range. G.S. Benkunsky recollected:

Monotonous droning of the engines… We are using the radiocompass less and less, gradually switching to wireless bearings, which are received by our radio operator Glazkov regularly giving us a chance to fly without deviation from the route. So in the strained work we imperceptibly pass Oymyakon, Berelekh, and now in the breaks of clouds we see Seymchan, where we were supposed to land. But having estimated the remaining fuel and having received weather report in Markovo we decide to fly over Seymchan to Markovo. Glazkov keeps regular radio communication with the ground, and in the allotted time he contacts Moscow directly. On the whole everybody is engaged in his own job. My co-pilot Kolya Maksimenko is making records in the logbook; Pasha Borisov is controlling the engine's running.

---

[48] G.S. Benkunsky, "SSSR-SShA: sorok shest let nazad," [The U.S.S.R.-U.S.A.: Forty Six Years Ago], *Civil Aviation*, 1991, no. 1, pp. 31-34.

Approximately an hour before arriving in Markovo, Glazkov received a radio message about landing of Allied troops in [North Africa]. Victor and I immediately come into the passenger cabin and passed the news to A.A. Gromyko and to other members of the delegation. The news caused exciting and happy reaction.[49]

After Markovo, the delegation flew to Uelkal, where they were forced to make an unscheduled layover. Alaska was covered with fog, making it impossible to fly on. The next morning they awoke to a white-covered world—hoarfrost, a frequent phenomenon in the area. The weather report was not encouraging. The entire shore on the Soviet side was covered with fog, but the weather in Alaska had improved and both Nome and Fairbanks were receiving flights. Late in the evening on August 18, the fog subsided a bit, allowing sufficient visibility for takeoff.

Alaska met them with fine weather. In Fairbanks they took aboard an American military pilot as well as a communication officer, who served as an interpreter. From Fairbanks they flew south through Canada and more inhabited areas. After nine more hours of flight, they landed in Edmonton. On the next day they crossed again into the United States. As Benkunsky recalled, once in the U.S., he flew the plane almost without the use of charts. In Fairbanks he had obtained information detailing the location of radio beacons across the U.S., so that he could precisely fly the route with the help of the radio and compass available on board. Benkunsky's crew did their job perfectly, and the Soviet delegation arrived at the conference on time.

In April 1945, the Soviet delegation headed by V.M. Molotov, along with delegations from Ukraine and Belorussia,[50] flew along the ALSIB to the United Nations International Conference in San Francisco. In May, along the same route, the delegation, after taking part in the UN General Assembly, was flown back to Moscow by crew from the 8th Transport Regiment. Other Soviet delegations, including those who took part in the International Aviation Conference in Edmonton, enjoyed the ALSIB's services. After the end of the war in Europe, the ALSIB route was abandoned as an international air route.

We Remember Those Remote Years

Soviets remember those isolated years during the long post-war era of the Cold War, when the Soviet and American veterans of the Alaska-Siberia Ferrying Route were separated from each other.

In June 1980, Thomas J. Watson, U.S. Ambassador to the U.S.S.R. from 1979 to 1981, was the first to express the idea of a memorial flight along the Alaska-Siberia route in a letter to I.P. Mazuruk. Watson's intent was to dedicate the action to mutual understanding between the Soviet and American people. Unfortunately, the political "weather" was non-flying at that time, even for outstanding pilots and diplomats.

Finally, in the summer of 1987, the seventy-three year old Watson, now a former diplomat, carried out his plan, and devoted his flight to the 45th anniversary of the opening of the Alaska-Siberia route. Before the flight, he expressed his confidence that his flight along the Siberian route would:

…remind everybody, both Russians and Americans, about our previous collaboration against the common enemy. The threat to both our countries in case of nuclear war unleashed deliberately or by accident is far more dangerous than the threat from the Nazi invasion. [51]

Watson flew his own airplane from the east coast of the U.S. to Moscow, where he was met by Mazuruk at the Sheremetyevo-2 airport. They had much to talk about. Watson invited Mazuruk to fly with him over the ALSIB and to share his joy in meeting with veterans of the route and visiting the places where they had endured so much. But old age prevented Ilya Pavlovich Mazuruk from

---

[49] Ibid., p. 32.

[50] Although Joseph Stalin demanded a vote for every Soviet republic in the General Assembly of the United Nations, he finally settled on extra votes for Ukraine and Byelorussia. [Editor].

[51] Ivan Negenblya's personal collection.

Women Aviators During World War II and on the Alaska-Siberia Airway

Miriam J. Lancaster
CAPT (Ret.) United States Public Health Service
Board of Directors/Alaska-Siberia Research Center

*Glamour, hell, it was hard work! My favorite word? Honor! Oh, honor! That to me
is more than a word. I mean, that's a way of life. I'd die for honor![1]*

Florence Shutsy-Reynolds (WASP 44-W-5)

American Women Pilots in World War II

In September, 1940, American pilot Jacqueline Cochran, famous for her speed records and flying awards, wrote Eleanor Roosevelt, urging her to carry forward the idea that women could fly in non-combat roles, releasing more men for combat duty.[2] American prejudice was strong against women pilots in the war and it took three years for Cochran's concept to gain voice, and another year for the idea to become reality.

In July 1941, Cochran presented a plan to Robert Lovett, Secretary of War for Air, and General "Hap" Arnold, Chief of the Air Force. In her presentation, Cochran detailed a program to use women pilots for ferrying aircraft. At that time, the Civil Aeronautical Administration had record of 2,733 licensed women pilots in the United States.[3] Of that cadre, 150 had over 200 flying hours and about 100 women had 300 or more hours. When queried, 130 women pilots said they were ready and eager to volunteer.[4] In Cochran's proposal, she pointed out that women were already successfully ferrying aircraft for the Royal Air Force in Great Britain, and that Soviet women were flying combat missions.

Many of the American women who already knew how to fly had been trained through the Civilian Pilot Training (CPT) program.[5] The Civil Aeronautics Act of 1938 provided the basis for establishing the CPT and President Roosevelt announced it on December 27, 1938. In an interview, Fairbanks resident Nancy Baker (WASP 43-W-4) recalled her CPT program at Bergen Junior College in Teaneck, N.J., where it was required that one out of every ten CPT trainees be female.[6]

In spite of this training, the male pilot shortage was so intense that, according to the military's own standards, men were called to fly who were physically unfit and overage. American women pilots were not utilized until Eleanor Roosevelt began speaking on the subject. Because of the pilot shortage and pressure from the First Lady, the tide of prejudice had begun to turn when, in her September 1, 1942, newspaper column titled "My Day," Mrs. Roosevelt wrote:

[1] Baylor University, "Wings Across America Interviews," Archive of WASP Interviews. Wings Across America project, 1819 River Street, Waco, Texas 76707; Kate Landdeck, "Not Just A Chorus Girl," *Woman Pilot*, July/August 2001, p. 16.

[2] Vera S. Williams, *WASPs: Women Airforce Service Pilots of World War II*. Motorbooks International, Osceola, WI, 1994, [hereinafter Williams, *WASPs*], p.19.

[3] Byrd Howell Granger, *On Final Approach: The Women Airforce Service Pilots of World War II*. Scottsdale: Falconer Publishing Company, 1991, p. 9.

[4] Ann B. Carl, *WASP Among Eagles: A Woman Military Test Pilot in World War II*. Washington D.C.: Smithsonian Institution Press, 1999 [hereinafter Carl, *WASP Among Eagles*], p. 36.

[5] Williams, *WASPs*, p. 20.

[6] Ibid., p. 20; Nancy L. Baker, personal interview with Miriam J. Lancaster, January 21, 2007.

This is not a time when women should be patient. We are in a war and we need to fight it with all our ability and every weapon possible. Women pilots, in this particular case, are a weapon waiting to be used.[7]

Two and a half months later, on November 15, 1942, following the extraordinary efforts of Jacqueline Cochran and Nancy Harkness Love, the first American women reported for flight training and took their oaths of allegiance.

Many roadblocks barred the establishment of women pilots within the American military. Tensions ran high between Jacqueline Cochran and Nancy Love, who held differing visions for women pilots' role in the war. Cochran and Love were vocal and each lobbied tirelessly for the military's acceptance of her own plan. On September 10, 1942, Nancy Love established the "Women's Auxiliary Ferrying Squadron" (WAFS). Angered over the acceptance of Love's plan, just six days later, on September 16, Cochran was appointed Director of the "Women's Ferrying Training Detachment" (WFTD), supervising all American women pilots connected to the Army Air Force (AAF). Her salary was $1 per year.[8]

J. Cochran's acceptance of this salary represented only one of several concessions that she made to get her plan accepted. Most importantly, she agreed that the women would be hired as civil servants rather than as military personnel. All along, though, Cochran planned for the women pilots to become militarized. Allowing their initial status as civil servants ameliorated fears she harbored that the war would "catch up" to them before she had had the chance to properly train the women pilots for military service. The idea was too new and no one knew how it would turn out. She felt that if she could just get "a foot

Jacqueline Cochran is credited with being the first woman to introduce the idea of a women's flying division within the Army Air Force. Courtesy of the Wings Across America project.

in the door" a militarization bill would follow. Cochran believed that red tape and Army bureaucratic channels would slow the process too much. In retrospect, Cochran said this line of thinking "backfired later, but at the time, it got us up and flying, off the ground."[9] On July 5, 1943, a consolidation of the WAFS and WFTD took place, and, on August 20, 1943, General Arnold issued the order to name the

---

[7] Carl, *WASP Among Eagles*, p. 36. "My Day" was a syndicated newspaper column (United Feature Syndicate, Inc.) published from 1935 to 1962. Mrs. Roosevelt wrote her column six days a week, interrupted only for four days when her husband died. "My Day" allowed the First Lady to reach millions of people, influencing greatly American thinking on social and political issues, as well as current and historical events.

[8] Deanie Bishop Parrish, (WASP 44-4), "WASP Timeline," *WASP On The Web: WASP Resources*, 1999, [hereinafter Parrish, "WASP Timeline"], p. 12. http://www.wingsacrossamerica.us/wasp/resources/timeline.htm

[9] Jacqueline Cochran and Maryann Bucknum, *Jackie Cochran*. Toronto-New York: Bantam Books, 1987, p. 200.

combined services Women Air-force Service Pilots (WASP).[10]

WASP Performance

Some call the WASP an elite group of women; but that was never a part of Cochran's plan. As explained by Ann Carl:

> *Her group would be businesslike, well organized, fair, and proficient. Their training would be, in fact, the same training Air Force cadets got — same airplanes, same hours, same ground school...regardless of former experience. They would, in fact, be professionals, the first such women flyers. So, not only did they benefit the war effort, but they received training for a new profession. Every WASP would, in fact, have gladly served as a WASP without pay...[11]*

Nancy Harkness Love established the Women's Auxiliary Ferrying Squadron on September 5, 1942. Courtesy of the Wings Across America project, Baylor University.

Overall, 25,000 young women jumped at the chance to fly planes as a WASP to help in the war effort. Very few of them fulfilled the basic requirements: to be an American citizen, be between 21 and 35 years old, have approximately 200 flying hours (later it would be less), be able to pass a stiff Air Force physical exam, and, most important, satisfy in an interview Cochran's pattern of what a future WASP should be. Only 1,800 were selected, and, of them, 1,070 would graduate.[12]

Initially there was no suitable base available for the training of women pilots, so the municipal airport at Houston, Texas, was used briefly. Then, early in 1943, the Flying Training Command left Avenger Field at Sweetwater, Texas. That allowed the WASP training program to be transferred to that location where it remained until the WASP were disbanded.

Equipment provided for WASP training tended to be surplus and/or obsolete, along with planes of various civilian types. This made training difficult and maintenance a challenge. The program used over 200 airplanes including PT-17s, PT-19s, BT-13s, BT-15s, AT-6s, AT-I7s, UC-78s, UC-43s, and UC-81s.[13]

Military training included protocol, courtesy and customs, Articles of War, safeguarding military information, drill and ceremonies, Army orientation, organization, military correspondence, chemical

---

[10] Williams, *WASPs*, p. 23. The WASP acronym created more than a little grammatical and spelling confusion. Often, an extra "s" is added to the acronym, which is incorrect. Adding the extra "s" is redundant because the title is already plural; and, the extra "s" spells "Pilotss." Additionally, the title is "Women Airforce Service Pilots," not "Women's Airforce Service Pilots." Adding an apostrophe to women makes the word possessive, meaning that the Airforce belongs to the women, which, of course, it does not.

[11] Carl, *WASP Among Eagles,* pp. 38-39.

[12] Ibid., pp. 38-39.

[13] Jacqueline Cochran, *Final Report on Women Pilot Program.* Dwight D. Eisenhower Library Archives, 200 S.E. Fourth St., Abilene, TX 67410 [hereinafter Cochran, *Final Report*], p. 15.

warfare, and personnel affairs. Ground school included mathematics, physics, map and chart reading, navigation, principles of flight, engines and propellers, weather, code, instrument flying, communications, and physical and first aid. Flight training started on lighter type planes and moved to faster, heavier types in the later weeks of each training session.

Initially, 23 weeks were spent in training, with 115 hours of flying and 180 hours of ground school. By the end of the war, training had been lengthened to 30 weeks, with 210 hours of flight time and 393 hours of ground school—generally, the same primary, basic, and advanced training required of male pilots.[14]

Cochran had to constantly defend the training program. It was commonly believed that, due to women's more delicate physical constitution, propensity to hysteria, menstruation, and potential pregnancy, women pilots would have a higher "wash-out" rate in training than male pilots undergoing the same training. This did not prove to be the case. Of the 1,830 women who were accepted for training, 35.5% were eliminated compared to the 35.6% elimination rate of male pilot trainees. Absenteeism was not a problem either. At the Sweetwater training facility, the six women instructors lost less time on the job than their male instructor counterparts.[15]

While many of the WASP were significantly shorter than male pilots, this posed little difficulty; they sat on their parachutes, and some of the women brought along extra pillows. In footage from the 1944 documentary *We Were WASP*,[16] one can see WASP walking to their planes wearing parachutes

"[WASP] study more diligently than male aviation cadets who proceeded them at Avenger Field, according to instructors. If marks are low, students have extra study halls in the evening to catch up. Trainees above are in meteorology class, learning to read symbols and weather maps of the sort that they will use as ferry pilots." Courtesy of Life *magazine, July 19, 1943, p. 75. Life® used by permission of* Life, *Inc. via Alexander Dolitsky.*

---

[14] Ibid., p. 14.

[15] Ibid., pp. 14, 15, 22.

[16] *We Were WASP*, producers Yvonne "Pat" Pateman and Gene Wyall, 1352nd Audio-Visual Squadron, Norton AFB. CA, WASP WWII Inc., 1990.

"'Stratosphere Twist' is the nickname students at Avenger Field have given to this calisthenics maneuver. In order to slow-roll Army trainers and do other acrobatics, it is important that students build up strong leg and arm muscles. Exercises they do in mass drill have been developed by the Air Force particularly to strengthen strategic muscles in fliers." Courtesy of Life *magazine, July 19, 1943, p. 79.* Life® *used by permission of* Life, Inc. *via Alexander Dolitsky.*

and carrying extra pillows. Nancy Baker remembers that during the time she was ferrying her P-47 Thunderbolts, she would sometimes hear reports of a plane flying without a pilot. In fact, it was 5'2" Baker who was so short she couldn't be seen from outside the cockpit of the heavy pursuit plane.[17]

In her final report, Cochran commented on the women's stamina and physical abilities:

WASP were subjected to every extreme of weather and oftentimes to being pushed in training to catch up hours so that classes could be regularly begun and graduated, the cases of either operational or flying fatigue were outstandingly low…WASP in ferry work lost less time than their male colleagues in the same work…Many of the WASP flew as much as 70 hours per month, a large part of which was in night flying, with no complaints except they wanted to fly more…It has been the opinion of many that women lack the muscular strength to do all types of flying…WASP flew the Fortresses for more than 12,500 hours with no fatalities and with only three minor accidents. WASP flew the even larger B-29…Early in the training program, it was not uncommon to have the trainees arise for ground school at 0800 after flying until 0400 in the morning. On the advice of the medical officer a rule was adopted that eight hours should intervene for sleep between ground school and flying activities.[18]

---

[17] Nancy L. Baker, interview with Miriam J. Lancaster, January 21, 2007.

[18] Cochran, *Final Report*, pp. 28-32.

The WASP proved to be safe pilots and set safety records in military flying. As stated in a January 1944 press release, "[The WASP] flew the equivalent of 3,000,000 miles for each fatal accident, the war department disclosed. Their present rate is .05 fatal accidents for each 1,000 hours of flying while the over-all fatality rate in the United States for the air forces is .07."[19]

"During the life of the WASP program there were 402 airplane accidents. Thirty-five of these, or 9% of the total, were fatal. Among AAF male flyers during the same period 11% of all accidents were fatal accidents. WASP fatalities numbered 38." [20]

After graduation, the women were assigned as ferry pilots in various locations, from factories to air fields, including commands where they towed targets behind their planes at which gunners shot live ammunition. Others were test pilots, flying new planes on their first-ever flights, as well as test-flying planes that had crashed or were malfunctioning in some way, and were just back from repair.[21]

Prejudice, Equality, and Rights

Today, as we progress toward gender equality, the disparities endured by the WASP may seem unconscionable. Men were hired from civilian flying jobs for a 90-day trial, after which they were commissioned into the Air Force with full military and officer rights, pay, and benefits. Women pilots were hired as provisional Civil Service employees. Men were paid $380 and women $250 per month.[22] WASP did not receive special income tax deductions that were allowed military men. The women had to pay their own way to training in Texas; and, once they arrived at Avenger Field, their room and board came out of their monthly training salary of $150 per month. While the number of flying hours required to enter WASP training varied as the program progressed, initially Colonel William Tunner, administrative officer of the Air Transport Command (ATC), required that women have 500 hours of flight time, be high school graduates, and be between 21 and 35 years of age. Male candidates were only required to have 200 hours of flight time, three years of high school, and be between 19 and 45 years of age to qualify.[23]

The WASP learned early on that the disparities ran deeper than rights, benefits, pay, and training requirements. Just four days after establishment of the WASP, a woman pilot was assigned to escort the body of another WASP who had been killed while delivering a military plane. When the escorting WASP requested the usual funeral escort funds, she was told that since she was not military, funds would not be made available to defray her expenses. On August 4, 1943, when a trainee was killed after she bailed out and her parachute failed to open, the WASP escort was able to use donated funds to accompany the body home; by this time, the trainees themselves were contributing to a fund so that a woman pilot escorting a body home did not have to pay her own expenses. At times, Jackie Cochran paid to ship the bodies home.[24] Male pilots' burial, escort costs and family benefits were fully funded by the military; however, the WASP killed in service received no benefits. Families of the deceased women pilots received no American flag and were not allowed to display the Gold Star, nor could their mothers join the Gold Star mothers' organization.[25]

---

[19] Williams, *WASPs*, p. 10.

[20] Cochran, *Final Report*, p. 23-24; Baylor University, "Wings Across America Interviews," Archive of WASP Interviews, Wings Across America. 1819 River Street Waco, Texas 76706. In WASP literature, there is some disagreement as to how many WASP died. The number generally varies between 33 to 38 casualties. This difference is attributed to how the deaths were tallied. In some cases, WASP deaths were counted only if they were the pilots, while other counts included them if they were passengers or acting as co-pilots to male pilots. Some include the instructors to the WASP pilots in fatal crashes, while others do not.

[21] Williams, *WASPs*, p. 10.

[22] War Department, Bureau of Public Relations, Press Release, August 8, 1944, pp 7-8.

[23] Deborah G. Douglas, *American Women in Flight Since 1940*. Lexington: The University Press of Kentucky, 2004, p. 81; Cindy Lash, "Fayette woman tells story of females flying on the WWII home front," *Pittsburg Post Gazette*, Local News, November 11, 2002, [hereinafter Lash, "Fayette woman"], p. 3.

[24] Williams, *WASPs*, p. 39.

[25] Lash, "Fayette woman," p. 3; Williams, *WASPs*, p. 141.

At Eleanor Roosevelt's urging, the president passed the G.I. Bill of Rights on June 22, 1944 providing for the education and training of returning veterans. Ironically, the women whom Mrs. Roosevelt had supported and encouraged to join the war effort were not allowed to claim veterans' health or education benefits.

Negative comments and gossip created a difficult environment for the women pilots. The May 29, 1943, issue of the Saturday Evening Post that featured Norman Rockwell's American icon, "Rosie the Riveter," initially helped pave the way for the newly formed WASP. Quickly, however, negative opinions of the women aviators began to emerge. Drew Pearson, a noted columnist who was openly critical of the program, waged a campaign from March through June of 1944 demanding deactivation of the WASP. Many Americans believed what Drew Pearson wrote. President Roosevelt, who held Pearson in low regard, did not. He once wrote in a letter to General Patrick J. Hurley that Pearson's "ill-considered falsehoods have come to the point where he is doing much harm to his own Government and to other nations. It is a pity that anyone anywhere believes anything he writes."[26] Unfortunately, powerful military and congressional leaders did believe Drew Pearson, along with other reporters and columnists who held similar views. Because the WASP were ordered not to defend themselves or even respond to the vicious attacks, the media's misrepresentations, for the most part, went unchallenged.

It was in this climate that the WASP militarization bill was brought before Congress. Not surprisingly, on June 21, 1944 (an election year), the bill was defeated in a vote of 188 to 169. Future training classes were canceled, and on June 26, 1944, a House of Representatives report recommended immediate discontinuance of the program. On December 20, 1944, the WASP ceased to exist.

"We were disbanded before the war was over," recalled Violet Thurn Cowden, WASP Class 43-W-4. "The planes we had been assigned to deliver were sitting with no one to deliver them. These planes were still needed to win the war," a war that was far from over, despite American optimism. In Europe, the Battle of the Bulge, Hitler's major counter-offensive against allied forces, began four days before the WASP were sent home.[27]

Late in December 1944, WASP records were classified and sealed, and remained archived and closed for over thirty years. The WASP role in the Allied victory largely went unrecorded. Few Americans knew of their contributions or even that the WASP ever existed.

Women were not again allowed to fly planes for the military until 1977,[28] after an early 70s resurgence of action to gain the right for American women to fly in the military. In the course of that effort, the contributions of the WASP in World War II were finally brought to light. Subsequently, led by Senator Barry Goldwater, many WASP, and others, Congress passed a bill to provide military status for modern women pilots, as well as for the WASP. Even in the 1970s it was a bitter battle. Once again, powerful groups, such as the American Legion and Veterans Administration, lobbied against the women, and were especially opposed to the WASP gaining retroactive military status. Despite the opposition, on November 3, 1977, President Jimmy Carter signed the bill. While it was too late to benefit from the G.I. Bill, WASP were granted the right to be buried in veterans' cemeteries on a space available basis.[29]

Now, through the WWII WASP Museum[30] and other programs such as Baylor University's "Wings Across America" and Texas Woman's University's oral history project,[31] surviving WASP are being

---

[26] Don Lohbeck, *Patrick J. Hurley*, Franklin D. Roosevelt on Pearson, in letter to General Patrick J. Hurley, August 30, 1943. Chicago: Regency Co., 1956, pp. 198-201.

[27] Laura Resnick, *Shot Down: The Women Airforce Service Pilots and the U.S. Media,* Association for Education in Journalism and Mass Communication, Toronto, Canada, 2004, p. 12.

[28] Williams, *WASPs*, p. 9.

[29] Parrish, "WASP Timeline," p. 24; Carl, *WASP Among Eagles*, p. 111; Williams, *WASPs*, p. 135.

[30] National WASP WWII Museum, 210 Loop 170, Sweetwater, TX.

[31] Texas Woman's University, Oral History Collection, The Women's Collection, Blagg-Huey Library.

interviewed and their memories documented, digitized, and published to preserve their remarkable histories.[32]

WASP and the Alaska-Siberia Airway

Between 1942 and 1945, when nearly 8,000 Lend-Lease aircraft were flown from their points of manufacture to Great Falls, Montana, many were flown by WASP who, once there, handed off the planes to male pilots. From Great Falls, men then flew the aircraft on across Canada to the Army's Ladd Airfield in Fairbanks, Alaska. There, Soviet pilots took over and flew the planes the remaining miles across Alaska and Siberia to the Russian front.

WASP Celia Hunter, in a speech to college students in 1997, described her experiences:

> *Women pilots ferried planes all over the U.S., but the U.S. Ferrying Division decided that women should not be allowed to ferry military planes any farther north than Great Falls, Montana. We ferried them from factories clear across the U.S., but "sorry, gals, turn them over to the men here," and they got to fly them on the Northwest Staging Route through Edmonton, Ft. Nelson, Watson Lake, and Whitehorse, to Fairbanks.*[33]

After the WASP were disbanded, Celia Hunter and another WASP, Ginny Wood, flew to Alaska on their own. Both women remained in Alaska, where they lived remarkable lives devoted to conservation and the environment. Celia Hunter died at the age of 82, on December 1, 2002.

Just a few days before her death, Celia described to John Binkley, in an interview for the *Fairbanks Daily News-Miner*, what it was like to fly a Bell P-39 Airacobra: "The aircraft, manufactured by Bell, had the engine mounted behind the cockpit. A 37mm gun stuck out the propeller nose cone, earning the plane the nickname, the 'flying cannon.'" Hunter also said that the women called this plane the "Bell from Hell." The P-39s quickly overheated, so ground crew often sprayed down the engines with hoses. They rattled so much, said Hunter, that she had to steady the instrument panel with one foot so she could read the gauges.[34]

An Interview with Ginny Hill Wood (WASP 43-W-4)[35]

During the war, Ginny Hill Wood was assigned to the 6th Ferrying Group in Long Beach, California. In an interview, she emphasized her motivation—she "just wanted to fly."

> *We didn't feel like we did anything special. It was simply a matter of being at the right place, at the right time, and the fact that I had good genes. If I didn't have good eyesight, I'd have been making planes instead of flying them. World War II was a citizens' war. Everyone was involved and we didn't complain. Whether it was rationing or flying, we did what needed to be done.*

During the Lend-Lease years, Wood flew "the planes with the red star" (the P-39s and the P-63s), from the factory near Buffalo, N.Y., to Great Falls, Montana, where the planes were turned over to male pilots. "Our status was in question, so they didn't want women flying over a foreign country—Canada," she laughed.

Wood called the P-39 a "short fuse" and the P-63 a "long fuse." While she never had to parachute from a plane, Wood deemed the P-39 the easiest to bail out of in an emergency.

[32] Baylor University, "Wings Across America Interviews," Archive of WASP Interviews. 1819 River Street, Waco, TX 76706.

[33] Celia Hunter, "My Alaska: A Personal Encounter," Linfield College. The Jane Claire Dirks-Edmunds Endowed Ecology Lectureship, McMinnville, Oregon, October 6, 1997.

[34] Sam Bishop, "Alaska-Siberia center commemorates regional cooperation," *Fairbanks Daily News-Miner*, February 8, 2002.

[35] Ginny Hill Wood, interview with Miriam J. Lancaster, December 10, 2006.

Fortunately, I never had to bail out, but if necessary, you only had to open the door. Once open, the door blew off in the wind, and then all you had to do was step out, just like you'd step out of a car. Some of the planes were more difficult because of all the wires and how they were made. Pilots even had to turn upside-down to bail out of some planes. But the P-39s were easy.

The planes we flew were all fresh from the factory. Every one of them had little things wrong with them. One time, when the P-63s were new, they had me take 3 short flights before leaving with the new plane. "How'd it fly?" they asked after my third flight. "Kind of wobbly," I said. I'd noticed it flew funny, but, being a new plane, I didn't think

Ginny Wood stands beside a P-63 King Cobra, in a photo taken in 1944 at one of the stops between Buffalo, NY and Great Falls, MT. She is wearing her parachute, which the pilots sat on when in the cockpit. Wood commented that some of the WASP were so short that they had to sit on extra pillows, but she was tall enough that the parachute was adequate for her. Courtesy of Ginny Hill Wood.

much of it, so I took off for Great Falls. Soon I was radioed to return. Someone in the tower noticed that the wing tanks were not secured — they forgot to put on the side braces and they were swaying precariously. That was really the only close call I had.

Once, we were grounded for five days somewhere in Illinois, around Chicago. They said there was sabotage somewhere — something had been put in our gas tanks, sugar. We never knew what it was really all about. But we had to stay with our planes for all five days.[36]

When we picked up our planes from the factory they made us sign that we had our maps, parachute, and a revolver. I always signed that I had it, but I never carried the revolver. I guess if we went down and the enemy got us we were supposed to shoot them. But, we were only flying in the states, and I thought carrying a revolver was silly.

We flew alone in the fighter planes. You couldn't use instruments because the guns covered them. They had instruments — you just couldn't see them. We did our own navigating and sometimes it was difficult to know where we were. During the war they took the town names off of railroad station roofs. They didn't want the enemy to know where they were; but that meant we didn't know either. Sometimes, I couldn't tell what state I was in because there were no landmarks. I rarely got lost, though — I was good at geography.

Alluding to the particular roles of the WASP versus the male pilots, Wood explained why the WASP disbandment ultimately hurt the war effort:

The women were trained to fly every kind of airplane that the Army had. The men were generally trained on only one plane. They were trained to fight, and they did that very well. But we flew everything. Once I flew ten different planes before I flew the same kind again. We just adapted. The Army liked the

---

[36] This memory is similar to that of Ann Carl (43-W-5), who recounted in her memoir *WASP Among Eagles*: "The first accident even Cochran believed was sabotage. The plane's engine quit and it crashed on its back on the runway. On examination, it was found that the fuel had been laced with sugar, which had stopped the engine. Unbelievably, this was hushed up…[The WASP then] began to check the airplanes they were to fly themselves, and they befriended the mechanics…," Carl, *WASP Among Eagles*, p. 51.

girls flying the fighter planes. We were small and fit in the cockpit better for the long flights. The men usually only flew short flights when fighting; but the ferrying flights were much longer. The fighter planes had a range of only about three hours for combat, but we ferried them in eight-hour stints.

When asked if she knew Jackie Cochran, Wood replied:

Yes. Well, a lot has been written about her and there's no need to go into all that. That's all pretty well known. She was aggressive, very political, and wanted to be a colonel. She wanted us to have equal status to the WACs. She was very ambitious. One thing I'll say for her is that she came up the hard way. I guess she was an orphan and didn't even get to go to school until she was about 10 years old. She had to fight for everything she got. And she wanted to get us militarized. But we didn't give a fiddle-dee-dee about all that rank and saluting. The enlisted men didn't have to salute us and I really liked it that way. The man out servicing my plane didn't have to salute me. He would have been in the plane instead of me if his eyesight was better. I had good eyesight and that's why I got to be a pilot. Cochran didn't like me very much.

Wood admired Nancy Love, whose style she contrasted with Cochran's:

She was a neat person. When she landed she just got out of her plane and filled out her flight plan, and that was it. When Jackie Cochran flew in, she radioed ahead and expected special attention. We didn't care for that.

Wood also remembers well the circumstances surrounding the final days of the WASP:

In 1944, Congress started asking, "Why are we paying the girls when the guys are coming home?" We were disbanded five months before the war ended. There was a whole field of planes waiting to be flown. But the guys weren't checked-out to fly all those different kinds of planes. They only knew the one fighter plane they'd been trained on. We flew everything and had flown them throughout the war. We offered to stay on and fly for $1 a month. But, there was political hanky-panky. Those guys in Congress were sitting there on their fat asses and didn't know what was going on. So, it was all over for us.

I always wanted to go to Alaska. I'd heard so much about it from the pilots flying there. So when I got home, and had the opportunity to fly a war surplus plane from Seattle to Fairbanks, I was happy to take the job. It wasn't military-owned anymore. A private person had purchased the plane. We flew it up to Fairbanks. It was about 50 below zero and we couldn't find a plane to

Ginny Wood (left) and an unidentified pilot stand beside a Boeing B-17 Flying Fortress, 1944. Courtesy of Ginny Wood via Alexander Dolitsky.

Ginny Wood stands beside a Northrop P-61 Black Widow (night fighter, radar equipped), 1944. Courtesy of Ginny Wood.

fly home in that weather. So, we stayed the winter. I never meant to stay, but I did, and just never left Alaska.

When asked about her most memorable experiences as a WASP, Ginny Wood simply answered,

The camaraderie. I loved that. And the planes — I loved checking out the new planes. We took very good care of them and never did any fancy flying. We never took risks and were very careful. We wanted to turn them over to the fighter pilots in good condition so the guys got a good plane.

An Interview with Ellen Campbell (WASP 44-W-7)

Ellen Campbell now lives in Juneau, Alaska, with her husband, Charles, whose voice exudes pride when he talks about his wife and her accomplishments as a WASP. He minimizes his own wartime accomplishments in France, preferring to focus on his wife, to whom he has been married for 58 years.

Ellen, too, tends to minimize her experiences as a WASP, preferring to talk about the "real" heroes who flew the planes across Alaska and Siberia to the front, the fighter pilots, and especially the Soviet women fighter pilots.

At the age of 19, Ellen learned to fly, so when the opportunity arose, she wanted to join the WASP. After graduation from WASP training, she was assigned to Columbus Army Air Force Base near Jackson, Mississippi, where she flew for the maintenance division as a test pilot.

If a plane was wrecked, it was repaired, if possible. Then, before it was returned to service, it had to be flown and tested out to see if it was repaired properly, and flyable. We also tested out the new planes.

Ellen Campbell in a Beech AT-10 Wichita, 1944. This plane was an important twin-engine trainer made of wood, except for the nose, cockpit and engine cowlings. Courtesy of Ellen Campbell via Alexander Dolitsky.

They had to be flown before they could be delivered. Those are the things I did as a test pilot. I flew the twin-engine AT-10 and other AT models. I also co-piloted B-25s. Some WASP flew experimental planes, but I didn't.

WASP also towed targets behind their planes while the boys shot live ammunition at them. Towing targets was dangerous and sometimes planes took direct hits. The girls who towed targets put their lives at risk. WASP died doing this.[37]

Many humorous things happened during that time. My best friend once had to make a forced landing in a cow pasture. We were taught that if something like this ever happened, we were to cut-off the engine and run, because the plane will likely explode. As she started to run from the plane, cows began walking toward her. She turned around and ran back to the plane and jumped into the cockpit, thinking, "I'll take my chances in the plane."

We were willing to do all the things the guys thought were onerous. Our work allowed the men to be fighter pilots and ferry the planes to Alaska.

Some male instructors resented having to teach us. One threw chalk at us and was very unkind. We didn't mind the kidding – that's always present with anything new; but the hazing that they put us through was difficult. Once I asked for a different instructor because of it. Our Colonel insisted

[37] Williams, *WASPs*, pp. 93-96.

on courteousness, so we were always polite and positive. So I said, "I'm not saying that you're a bad instructor, but in order to learn, I need a different kind of instructor." My request was granted, and while the previous instructor promised to see that I washed out, the new instructor found that I passed everything on the checklist. He said the only thing he could provide negative comment on, was that my fingers were a little tremulous on the controls of the plane. But everything else was perfect.

I guess the things I would like my grandchildren to know about that time is that we had a patriotism that inspired us to take active part in winning the war. No matter what was asked of us, we went through it with joy, fortitude, and a relish for flying.

Ever since those memorable days of the WASP and the Russian/American joint effort, I have become increasingly aware of a truth that has grown even more strongly in these troubled and fear-filled days. All people are dear to God. We gain the victory when we come to the peace table and work together for the good of all. [38]

Soviet Women Combat Pilots

While the Women Air Service Pilots (WASP) had key figures like Jacqueline Cochran and Nancy Love who were central players in their organization and deployment, for the Soviet women pilots it was

Marina Raskova.[39] Raskova, one of over 800,000 WWII Soviet military women, was a folk hero who, as a navigator, set many world records during the 1930s. Raskova, already a Major in the Soviet Air Force by 1941, wielded sufficient political influence to persuade Joseph Stalin to form three regiments of women combat flyers. By December 1, 1941, these regiments had already been formed and trained for combat duty: the 586th Fighter Aviation Regiment, equipped with Yak-1 fighters; the 587th Short-Range Day Bomber Aviation Regiment, supplied with obsolete Su-2 bombers and later replaced with more sophisticated Pe-2 bombers; and the 588th Night Bomber Regiment, equipped with U-2 biplanes.[40]

During four years of war, these regiments flew a combined total of over 30,000 combat sorties, and produced 30 Heroes of the Soviet Union, among them two fighter aces Lidiya Litvyak (12 kills) and Katya Budanova (11 kills), the only women aces in history.[41] Most of the mechanics and bomb loaders in the 587th and the 588th Bomber Regiments and in the 586th Fighter Aviation Regiment were also women.[42]

Marina Raskova. Courtesy of Reina Pennington.

Of the three regiments, the 586th Fighter Aviation Regiment was the first female regiment to complete training and to take part in combat, beginning on April 16, 1942. Its first mission was to protect fixed targets near Saratov against enemy bombers. Although this was an important mission, it was not on the front lines of the war, so there was not much excitement or ceremony surrounding the 586th's departure from the training school. Later, however, the 586th would participate in 4,419 combat missions, with 125 air battles, and a total of 38 confirmed kills.[43]

The 588th Night Bomber Regiment, later known as the 46th Taman Guards Night Bomber Aviation Regiment, was a women-only combat regiment formed by Marina Raskova and led by Major Yevdokiya Bershanskaya. These night bombers flew harassment bombing missions from 1942 to the end of the war. Flying in obsolete wood and canvas Polikarpov Po-2 biplanes of a 1928 design that were originally intended for training and crop dusting, forty two-person crews flew more than 23,000

---

[38] Ellen Campbell, personal interview with Miriam J. Lancaster, January 9, 2007.

[39] Reina Pennington, "The Pioneers: Maria Raskova and the Soviet Women Pilots of World War II," [hereinafter Pennington, "The Pioneers"], 2002, p. 3. http://www.cite.monash.edu.au/hargrave/soviet_women_pilots.html

[40] Reina Pennington, *Wings, Women, & War: Soviet Airwomen in World War II Combat*, [hereinafter Pennington, *Wings, Women, & War*], 2002. Norman: University Press of Kansas, p. 31.

[41] Ibid., p. 2; Vladimir Belyakov, "Russia's Women Top Guns," *Aviation History*, March 2002, p. 34.

[42] Pennington, "The Pioneers," p. 8.

[43] Ibid., p. 9; Pennington, *Wings, Women & War*, p. 49.

sorties, dropping as many as 3,000 tons of bombs. The plane could only carry 2 bombs that weighed less than a ton altogether. When the 588th received orders to go to the front, garrison commander Colonel Bagaev gave the following speech:

> *Today, for the first time, a women's regiment leaves our airfield for the front. You do not fly on awesome machines, but on training aircraft. And it's true that you yourselves are not excessively awesome in appearance. But I am certain that in these light-winged airplanes, you will be able to inflict heavy blows on the enemy. Let fly with you my fatherly wish: success to you and combat glory!*[44]

Indeed, they did inflict heavy blows to the enemy. The women carried two bombs in their planes per sortie, undertaking multiple night missions. Because of the limited range of the aircraft, such regiments were based very near the front so they could fly repeat missions. "On average, the Po-2 crews flew five to ten missions each night."[45] While their biplanes were obsolete and slow, the women pilots made daring use of their exceptional maneuverability. Accurate and deadly, the German pilots found them difficult to shoot down. Overall, each of the woman bomber pilots who survived the war in 1945 flew more than 1,000 missions. Their exemplary service earned the women pilots flight assignments in the final attack on Berlin. The women of the 588th/46th were so feared that the Germans called them *Nachthexen* (*Ночные Ведьмы*) — the Night Witches. The night bombers were the most highly-decorated units of the Soviet Air Force. Twenty-three *Nachthexen*, out of thirty produced by three women regiments, earned the Gold Star of the Hero of the Soviet Union.[46]

Katya Ryabova and Nadya Popova in a single night made 18 bombing sorties into enemy territory. Courtesy of Reina Pennington.

Legacy of the Soviet Women Pilots

Initially, Soviet women pilots endured prejudice and sexism similar to their American counterparts. Male pilots refused to fly with women "wingmen" and refused to fly airplanes repaired or serviced by women mechanics and ground crew. However, the courage and skill of the women proved their competence. Ultimately, without reservation, the entire Soviet Union praised their women pilots. Unlike their American sisters, thousands of honors and medals were awarded to the Soviet women pilots.

By the close of World War II, almost 1,000 Russian women had flown combat missions in every type of Soviet warplane. Aviation General-Colonel Vladimir Lavrinenkov confirmed that the women flew the same type of missions and performed as well as the men:

> *The women pilots served at the airfield on an equal footing with the men. And they even fought as well as the men… It was not easy for the girls at the front. Especially for women fighter-pilots: air combat demanded from them unusual physical strength and endurance. And the fact that the girls, without complaining, bore all the difficulties is a credit to them, and evoked tremendous respect from those around them.*[47]

---

[44] Ibid., p. 49.

[45] Ibid., p. 80.

[46] Pennington, "The Pioneers," p. 3; Pennington, *Wings, Women, & War*, p. 72.

[47] Vladimir Lavrinenkov, *Vozvrashchenie v nebo*, 2nd ed., Moscow: Voenizdat, 1983, pp. 56-57, quoted in Pennington, *Wings, Women & War*, pp. 161-162.

The success of Soviet women pilots, and in many cases their very existence, was kept secret in the West, not by the Soviets who publicly came to revere these women, but by the Americans and their Allies.[48]

Because of the Soviets' eventual unqualified acceptance of female pilots, and the fact that they served in combat in the U.S.S.R. and over Germany, it may seem logical to assume that female Soviet pilots ferried planes from Fairbanks along the Alaska-Siberia Airway; however, there is no record confirming this assumption. Ivan Yefimovich Negenblya, a Russian aviation historian from Yakutsk, Sacha Republic, states that women did not ferry planes on the Alaska-Siberia route and they did not hold positions

From left to right: Lydia Litvyak, Ekaterina Budanova, and Marina Kuznetsova of the all female 586th Fighter Aviation Regiment. Courtesy of Inna V. Pasportnikova via Reina Pennington.

of engineer-mechanics. Women did, however, serve as meteorologists and radio operators along the airway.[49]

We All Contributed to the War Effort

While there is no evidence that women pilots flew the Alaska-Siberia leg of the Lend-Lease flights from Great Falls, Montana, to Krasnoyarsk in Siberia, their contributions toward victory were enormous. Over the course of the war, the WASP delivered essential battle planes from their point of manufacture to Great Falls and to other locations. During their time of service, 38 WASP died and many were wounded in the line of duty. Their memoirs are an important legacy for us all. The efforts of Jacqueline Cochran and the determination of many WASP to place themselves on equal footing with male pilots set the foundation for the enhanced rights that women enjoy in American society today.

"In the line of duty, WASP flew a total of 60 million miles, or about 2,500 times around the earth at the equator."[50] Yet, WASP like Ginny Wood and Ellen Campbell believe they did nothing special. They would say, "It's not just the women pilots, it's everyone. We all contributed to the war effort. We were all equally important." They would point to women such as 93-year-old Irene Noyes, who lives in Fairbanks, Alaska, and remembers that she spent hours at a sewing machine, making wing covers for the Soviets and Americans at Ladd Field. She also repaired and packed parachutes and worked as a telephone operator on equipment that was so old she had to shout to be heard on long distance calls. She shouted so much, and so loudly, that she became hoarse.[51]

Many years after the war, Soviet pilot Nadia Popova said, "At night sometimes, I look up into the dark sky, close my eyes and picture myself as a girl at the controls of my bomber and think, 'Nadia, how on earth did you do it?'"[52]

In a December 11, 2006, National Public Radio (NPR) broadcast titled "Radio Diaries: An Oral History of the WASP," it was noted that of the original 1,074 WASP[53] only about 600 were thought to

[48] Roy McShane, *Hwelte: The Best Kept Russian Secret of WWII*, Writers Club Book, 2002.

[49] Ivan Yefimovich Negenblya, correspondence to Alexander Dolitsky, December, 6, 2006.

[50] Cochran, *Final Report*, p. 28.

[51] Dermot Cole, "For Lend-Lease effort she spent hours at work on sewing machine," *Fairbanks Daily News-Miner*, August 27, 2006.

[52] Pennington, "The Pioneers," p. 3.

[53] Williams, *WASPs*, p. 132.

be alive today.[54] Of those, most are in their 80s. Locating and interviewing these heroic women should be a high priority so that each can be honored in her own lifetime. Where possible, the same attempts should be made to contact and record Russian women pilots' memoirs as well. This documentation will serve as inspiration to future generations so that they can know of these women's dedication, perseverance, and ultimate acts of heroism.

Thanks to the novel efforts of these brave women, our daughters and granddaughters are freer to pursue their dreams and fully develop their talents. The WASP and Soviet women pilots of World War II paved the way for girls and young women to know that whatever their goals and aspirations, *the sky's the limit.*

Women Airforce Service Pilots (WASP) Shirley Slade on the cover of Life *magazine, July 19, 1943. Life® used by permission of* Life *Inc. via Alexander Dolitsky.*

---

[54] This number is corroborated as approximately accurate by Nancy Parish of Baylor University's Wings Across America project, who maintains WASP mailing lists. Wings Across America, 1819 River Street, Waco, Texas 76706.

Celebrating the Home Front in Fairbanks[1]

The World War II Alaska-Siberia Lend-Lease Memorial

Too often wars are described in terms of presidents and generals, emperors and kings, in grand strategy and elaborate campaigns. But wars affect the lives of all people—the soldiers who fight, and the women, children, and men who support the effort from home. The Lend-Lease program was a turning point during World War II, and an essential home-front undertaking.

On August 27th, 2006, representatives of several nations that had participated in the Alaska-Siberia Airway transport of warplanes celebrated the dedication of the WWII Alaska-Siberia Lend-Lease Memorial in Fairbanks, Alaska. This was a memorable event in Alaska, and we are grateful to everyone who contributed to the construction of the Memorial, and to the celebration, for his or her interest and support in preserving an essential chapter of Alaska's history.

Master of Ceremony John Binkley (right) and Program Manager Alexander Dolitsky (left) acknowledge distinguished guests at the WWII Alaska-Siberia Lend-Lease Memorial dedication, Fairbanks, Alaska, August 27th, 2006. Defense Dept. photo by U.S. Air Force Staff Sgt. D. Myles Cullen.

---

[1] Remarks and speeches are presented in this section in the same order that they were delivered at the WWII Alaska-Siberia Lend-Lease Plaza dedication in Fairbanks, Alaska, on August 19th, 2005, and at the WWII Alaska-Siberia Lend-Lease Memorial dedication in Fairbanks, Alaska, on August 27th, 2006.

Alaska House of Representatives

Richard Foster
P.O. Box 1630
Nome, AK 99762
907-443-5036
Fax 907-2162

During Session
State Capitol Rm. 410
Juneau, AK 99801-1182
907-465-3789
Fax 907-465-3242

Majority Whip

March 2001

To Whom It May Concern:

We, members of the Alaska House of Representatives, support the Alaska-Siberia Research Center (AKSRC) in their efforts to erect a monumental bronze sculpture commemorating the Lend-Lease program between the United States and Russia during World War II. See attached information.

[handwritten signatures]

Whitaker, 31

Kevin Meyer, 19

Drew Scalzi Dist 25

Lesil McGuire D-17

Mary Kapsner, 39

Ann Wolf D15

Harry Crawford -22

Sharon McCisina D21

Drew Scalzi -7

Norman Rokeberg D-11

Carl Moses -40

Lyman Hoffman -D-23

Pete Kott -D.24

Peggy Wilson -2

RePR Richard Foster

R Foster - Nome 38 district

Beth Kerttula - Juneau 3

Beth Kerttula

Rep. Lisa Murkowski - Anchorage -14

Bill Williams -1

Hugh Fate 733

Rep Hugh Fate

Mike Chenault -9

Rep Mike Chenault. Dist 9.

Rep. John P. Harris -35

Rep. Ken Lancaster -8

C. Morgan Aniak -36

Con Bunde -18

Joe -10

Bill Hudson -4

Alakanuk, Brevig Mission, Chevak, Elim, Emmonak, Gambell, Golovin, Hooper Bay, Kotlik, Koyuk, Mekoryuk, Mountain Village, Newtok, Nightmute, Nome, Pitka's Point, St. Mary's, St. Michael, Savoonga, Scammon Bay, Shaktoolik, Sheldon Point, Stebbins, Teller, Toksook Bay, Tununak, Unalakleet, White Mountain

Alaska House of Representatives support of the monumental bronze Lend-Lease sculpture. Courtesy of the Alaska-Siberia Research Center (AKSRC).

In the early 1990s, the Alaska-Siberia Research Center began its research on the World War II Lend-Lease Program, including interviews of program participants. Subsequently, the Center published many professional and popular articles on the subject.

The sculpture project began in 2000, and, after six years of hard work and creative endeavor, the magnificent WWII Alaska-Siberia Lend-Lease Memorial, a dramatic symbol of international cooperation against evil, was dedicated on August 27th, 2006.

Veterans' organizations, various public institutions, and individuals endorsed the project from the early stages of its development. Among them: President of the Russian Federation Vladimir V. Putin, Russian Ambassador to the United States Yuri Ushakov, Fairbanks North Star Borough, City of Nome, the Moscow Monino Aviation Museum, Institute of the North, Governor Walter Hickel, Governor Tony Knowles, City and Borough of Juneau, Interior Veterans Coalition, Veterans of Foreign Wars, Juneau Jewish Community, Villanova University,

Mikhail Chemiakin's proposed design of the Lend-Lease Memorial, 2002. Courtesy of AKSRC.

Alaska Geographic Alliance, and Sorbonne University of France. The Alaska State Legislature overwhelmingly passed House Joint Resolution 27 in 2001 in support of this project, and later appropriated significant funds for the construction of the Memorial Plaza. Additional support was provided by a grant from the Alaska Department of Transportation and Public Facilities. A substantial amount of funding for the construction of the Memorial also came from the U.S. Congress, in 2002, through an appropriation sponsored by U.S. Senator Ted Stevens.

The Center's Board of Directors, Alexander Dolitsky, John Binkley, William Ruddy, Robert Price, Miriam Lancaster, Dr. Anna Kerttula, Dr. Jeffrey Hahn, and Mead Treadwell have enthusiastically

Alaska-Siberia Lend-Lease Memorial Plaza, site plan, April 2003. Courtesy of AKSRC.

supported the project over the years by formulating the concepts of the Memorial, establishing guidelines and policies, reviewing various proposals, and conducting thorough research for the project.

Kevin Doniere, then Landscape Architect of Land Design North, Inc., Fairbanks, Alaska, developed the design concept for the Lend-Lease Memorial Plaza in April 2003, and Jim Loftus of PDC, Inc. Fairbanks, designed and constructed a granite plinth for the Memorial in 2005-2006.

From 2001 through 2003, the Center's Board received and reviewed proposals for the WWII Alaska-Siberia Lend-Lease Memorial from three well-known sculptors. The Russian sculptor Mikhail Chemiakin proposed a symbolic design for the Memorial. Chemiakin described his concept as follows:

> *My sculpture will consist of a ten-foot long sword descending from the heavens, its hilt made of the three blades of an airplane's propeller. The sword's point in the process of breaking a shield emblazoned with a swastika, in the grasp of an allegorical dragon symbolizing the evil of fascism. The dragon is reclining [on] a thirteen-foot high granite pedestal decorated with both abstract and figurative bronze and granite elements representing war, resistance, heroism, and US-Soviet wartime cooperation. While the central sculpture will be identical at all seven sites, each individual pedestal can be decorated with elements reflecting the history of Lend-Lease [operations] at each site, including names, maps, events, and local history.[2]*

The second proposal came from Alaskan sculptor Joan Bugbee Jackson of Cordova. Jackson is known for her WWII soldier-at-war statue erected in Anchorage on June 3, 2001. Her proposed design for the Lend-Lease Memorial in Fairbanks was titled "Winged Victory."

> *The proposed design consists of the classic figure of Winged Victory racing across the top of the world, showing the northern hemisphere in a raised map relief. She is in swift motion, rushing the planes to victory. Her urgent mission is to deliver over 8,000 planes made in the United States to the Russian front in WWII.*
>
> *Fairbanks, Alaska, was the point of transfer from U.S. hands to the Russian pilots. A star on the globe indicates this point of transfer. A bronze rod arches over the globe indicating the flight path of the planes and their stops en route.*
>
> *The figure of Victory is in the symbolic act of transferring a plane (a P-39), held high in her left hand, over to the figure of a Russian pilot (or some other symbol representing Russia) held in the her right hand. Her face is turned toward her right hand, focusing on the Russian pilot (or symbol) for whom the plane is intended. The statue is facing south so that the direction of her passing the plane is true to the east to west direction of the planes' flights.*

After comprehensive review of three proposals, the Board favored the traditional/realistic design for the Memorial in Fairbanks submitted by Juneau sculptor Richard T. Wallen. The Board believed that a figurative design would be the most appropriate for Fairbanks' demographic and cultural settings. In January of 2003, the Center commissioned Wallen for the job. In the course of his ar-

Joan Bugbee Jackson's proposed design of the Lend-Lease Memorial, 2003. Courtesy of AKSRC.

---

[2] Written correspondence with Mikhail Chemiakin, dated January 19, 2002, Dolitsky's private collection.

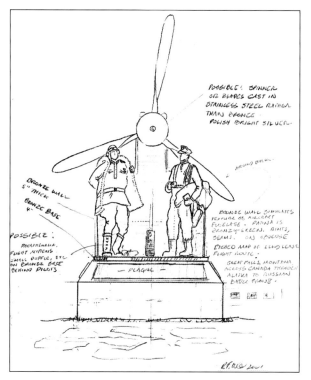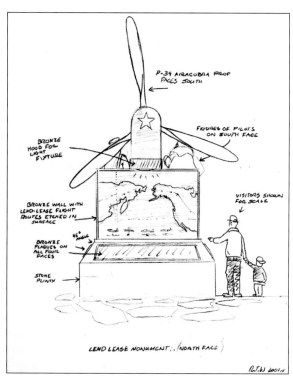

Richard T. Wallen's initial design of the Lend-Lease Memorial, 2001. Courtesy of AKSRC.

tistic work, the sculptor modified the original design of the monument as it is illustrated on the cover page of this book.

Having thoroughly researched the subject, the Center selected the Franklin D. Roosevelt quote for the Memorial, edited the four foot by six foot bronze plaque/map on the North face of the monument, and designed and implemented the two foot by three foot bronze plaques on the West, North, and East faces of the monument.

Alexander B. Dolitsky
Chairman/Project Manager
Alaska-Siberia Research Center
Juneau, Alaska

William G. Ruddy
President
Alaska-Siberia Research Center
Juneau, Alaska

STATE OF ALASKA

Executive Proclamation

by
Frank H. Murkowski, Governor

On May 9 all peaceful nations celebrate the anniversary of Victory Day over Nazi Germany and its European allies during World War II. The formal end of World War II came on September 2, 1945 with the Japanese government signing the surrender document on the battleship *Missouri* in Tokyo harbor, Japan. The Alaska-Siberia Lend-Lease Program significantly contributed to the victory of World War II.

The wartime Lend-Lease Act between the United States and Allied nations, including the Soviet Union, allowed 42 allied countries to provide "...mutual assistance in fighting a war against the aggression."

The Agreement included Alaska as the exchange point between the U.S. and the Soviet Union from 1942 to 1945. Nearly 8,000 aircraft were flown by the U.S. Army Air Corps 7th Ferrying Squadron from Great Falls, Montana, across various bases in Canada, to Army Ladd Airfield in Fairbanks, now Fort Wainwright. From Fairbanks, members of the Soviet Air Force piloted the planes across Alaska and Siberia to the Russian warfront. Due to the severe weather conditions and mechanical problems, 133 airplanes crashed in North America and 44 in Siberia along the Alaska-Siberia Airway.

The heroism of the American and Soviet pilots who flew these warplanes from the United States to the Soviet Union during World War II and all who participated in this endeavor will be always remembered.

NOW, THEREFORE, I, Frank H. Murkowski, Governor of the State of Alaska, do hereby proclaim September 2, 2006, as:

Alaska-Siberia Lend-Lease Day

in Alaska, and encourage all Alaskans to consider the importance of this program in helping achieve Allied victory against Nazi Germany and its Axis powers 61 years ago.

Dated: June 29, 2006

Frank H. Murkowski
Governor, who has also authorized the seal of the State of Alaska to be affixed to this proclamation.

Do the People Want a War?

Remarks by Alexander B. Dolitsky

Chairman/Project Manager of the Alaska-Siberia Research Center, Juneau, Alaska
World War II Alaska-Siberia Lend-Lease Memorial Plaza Dedication, Fairbanks, Alaska
August 19th, 2005

The Alaska-Siberia Research Center began this project nearly 5 years ago. With the help of many individuals, agencies and government organizations, we made great progress that will result in the erection of the Alaska-Siberia Lend-Lease Memorial in this park next year.

The Lend-Lease Program by the United States was the largest enterprise of the 20th Century. Truly, nearly $50 billion[3] worth of goods and services were delivered to 42 Allied countries during the four-year period, either under constant enemy attacks or severe weather conditions, or both.

It is significant that the Alaska-Siberia Lend-Lease Program demonstrated a remarkable effort of international cooperation of peace-seeking nations against evil—against Nazi Germany and its Axis powers. The Alaska-Siberia Lend-Lease Memorial will preserve awareness of that massive effort for the future.

I am going to recite the poetry of the Russian poet Yevgeniy Yevtushenko, titled *Khotyat li Russkiye Voiny? Do the Russians Want a War?* I have changed the word *Russians* to the word *People,* as it is more appropriate for this occasion.

Do the People Want a War?

Say, do the People want a war?
Go ask our land, then ask once more
That silence lingering in the air
Above the birch and poplar there.
Beneath those trees lie soldier lads
Whose sons will answer for their dads.
To add to what you learned before,
Say—Do the People want a war?

Those soldiers died on every hand
Not only for their own dear land,
But so the world at night could sleep
And never have to wake and weep.
New York and Paris spend their nights
Asleep beneath the leaves and lights.
The answer's in their dreams, be sure.
Say—Do the People want a war?

Sure, we know how to fight a war,
But we don't want to see once more
The soldiers falling all around,
Their countryside a battleground.
Ask those who give the soldiers life,
Go ask my mother, ask my wife,
Then you will have to ask no more,
Say—Do the People want a war?

Yevgeniy Yevtushenko, 1961.

---

[3] The $50 billion spent on Lend-Lease would be equivalent to around $700 billion in 2007.

World War II Alaska-Siberia Lend-Lease Memorial Plaza dedication, Fairbanks, Alaska, August 19th, 2005. Stone-setting ceremony. From left to right: Project Manager Alexander Dolitsky, Russian Consul-General Vladimir Volnov, Canadian Consul Karen Matthias, Russian Ambassador Yuri Ushakov, Alaska Governor Frank Murkowski, AKSRC Director John Binkley, Fairbanks North Star Borough Mayor Jim Whitaker, Fairbanks Mayor Steve Thompson, Alaska Senator Gary Wilken, North Pole Mayor Jeff Jacobson. Courtesy of AKSRC.

From left to right: Project Manager Alexander Dolitsky, Russian Consul-General Vladimir Volnov, Canadian Consul Karen Matthias, Russian Ambassador Yuri Ushakov, Alaska Governor Frank Murkowski, AKSRC Director John Binkley, Fairbanks North Star Borough Mayor Jim Whitaker, Fairbanks Mayor Steve Thompson, Alaska Senator Gary Wilken, North Pole Mayor Jeff Jacobson. Courtesy of AKSRC.

Canada's Role in the Alaska-Siberia Airway

Remarks by Karen Matthias
Canadian Consul, Anchorage, Alaska
WWII Alaska-Siberia Lend-Lease Memorial Plaza Dedication, Fairbanks, Alaska
August 19th, 2005

It is a great pleasure for me to be here in Fairbanks. Today, we are recognizing the extraordinary courage and dedication of the men and women who took part in the Alaska-Siberia route of the Lend-Lease program.

While this is primarily a connection between the United States and Russia, Canada had a small but important role in the program. Each of the thousands of planes that were flown up from the Lower 48 stopped for refueling and maintenance in Canada: in Calgary, Edmonton, Grande Prairie, Fort St. John, Fort Nelson, Watson Lake, Whitehorse and Snag.

Canada had joined the war effort in 1939. By 1945, 1.1 million Canadians had served in the armed forces; that was 10% of the population of approximately 11.5 million. So, Canadians were very closely affected by the war and well aware of the importance of the Lend-Lease program. I would like to think that when the American pilots landed in those Canadian cities and towns that they were warmly welcomed as family and thanked for their bravery and service to the cause.

Canada and the United States share a long tradition of cooperation in defending our continent and fighting for freedom at home and in the rest of the world. The United States is Canada's most important ally and defence partner, and we have one of the most effective and integrated defence relationships in the world. Canada stands with the United States in the battle against terrorism and in defense of the common values and political ideals that bind us.

I believe this memorial will be a popular destination for visitors and locals in Fairbanks and it will keep strong the memory of the men and women who gave so much for freedom in the Second World War.

Thank you.

Canadian Consul Karen Matthias speaks at the World War II Alaska-Siberia Lend-Lease Memorial Plaza dedication, Fairbanks, Alaska, August 19th, 2005. Courtesy of AKSRC.

The World War II Lend-Lease Memorial Is a Tribute to "The Greatest Generation"

Remarks by Yuri V. Ushakov
Russian Ambassador to the United States, Washington, D.C.
WW II Alaska-Siberia Lend-Lease Memorial Plaza Dedication, Fairbanks, Alaska
August 19th, 2005

Dear Mr. Governor,
Dear friends,
Dear countrymen,

First of all, thank you for this opportunity to join you at this dedication ceremony for the Alaska-Siberia Lend-Lease Memorial.

This year the world commemorates the 60th anniversary of the end of World War II. That's why it is very symbolic and very timely that we have gathered here to celebrate one of the most glorious chapters in the history of Russian-American wartime alliance.

As you are aware, on the 9th of May, over 50 world leaders came to Moscow's Red Square to celebrate VE Day. It was indeed a joint celebration of our common victory forged by the entire anti-Hitler coalition, by all Allies.

The Russian people who had to shoulder the greatest burden and suffered the most losses in that war also remember that thousands of American GIs sacrificed their lives to defend the liberty of mankind.

The opening of the second front in 1944 came as a long-awaited help

Russian Ambassador to the United States Yuri Ushakov speaks at the World War II Alaska-Siberia Lend-Lease Memorial Plaza dedication, Fairbanks, Alaska, August 19th, 2005. Courtesy of AKSRC.

to the Russian troops who had to counter single-handedly the invading Nazi armadas and then to liberate the occupied territories. But, in a broader sense, the second front was opened two years earlier when President Roosevelt responded to the Russian request by launching an unprecedented program of military and food supplies to assist our war effort.

During the war, Russian soldiers and officers on the front-line knew what a difference was made by the arrival of American planes, tanks, jeeps, weapons, canned meat and other vital supplies. We are mindful of the fact that Alaska played a key role in the Lend-Lease Program, with nearly eight thousand warplanes being delivered to the Eastern Front through Fairbanks between 1942 and 1945. That effort came not only as crucial military assistance but also provided to the Russian army and the

Russian people much needed moral support.

I believe that today nobody doubts that the outcome of World War II would have been different, had Russia not sacrificed 27 million lives. As President Bush once admitted when talking about the significance of Russia's war effort: "If not for Russia, none of this would have happened."

At the same time, it would also be appropriate to remind the younger generation both in Russia and the United States of the significance of the supply route between Alaska and the Russian Far East, which was part of the American Lend-Lease Program.

For example, in Russia everybody knows our most famous pilot and war hero Alexander Pokryshkin, but few still remember that, during most of his winning air battles, he flew American Airacobras with red stars painted on them. Likewise, not many people in this country know that there was an American by the name of Joseph Beyerly who escaped from a Nazi concentration camp and continued his fight as a crewman in a Russian tank.

That is why we appreciate the initiative put forward by the Alaska-Siberia Research Center and supported by Alaska's governor, by Senator Ted Stevens, the Mayor of Fairbanks, and of course by Alexander Dolitsky and John Binkley to commemorate this glorious chapter in the history of Russian-American wartime cooperation by creating a memorial to Lend-Lease.

This monument will not only serve as a tribute to "The Greatest Generation," but, like the famous photo of a handshake of a Russian and American soldier over a broken bridge across the Elbe River at the end of the war, it will always be a reminder to all of us that Russians and Americans were brothers-in-arms in the course of that war against a common enemy.

The example of our wartime alliance continues to guide us in the 21st Century. Six decades later, the unity demonstrated by the Russian and American people during the war is still important to us. The lessons of that war are also not to be forgotten in view of the threats and challenges of today. These lessons call on us to build such a relationship between our nations that would make us not only partners but true Allies as we were during the war.

Russian Ambassador to the United States Yuri Ushakov is greeted by Russian folk singers during a reception at Lavelle's Bistro Restaurant, Fairbanks, Alaska, August 26th, 2006. Photo: Sergei Maurits.

I am pleased to note that Russia and the United States work closely together on the most urgent issues facing the world community. At times, we may have different approaches to tackling certain problems, but our strategic goals across the spectrum of international politics are identical. We also share the same democratic values and principles.

In conclusion, I would like to express once again my profound gratitude to those who made this event happen. The State of Alaska and the City and Borough of Fairbanks do deserve the Lend-Lease Memorial. No doubt that unveiling of the completed Memorial will be a success next year. And I am sure that many prominent guests will come here from all over the world to take part in this great celebration.

Good luck and best wishes to all of you.

We Flew in the Same Sky

Remarks by Alexander B. Dolitsky

Chairman/Project Manager of the Alaska-Siberia Research Center, Juneau, Alaska
World War II Alaska-Siberia Lend-Lease Memorial Dedication, Fairbanks, Alaska
August 27th, 2006

Dear friends and distinguished guests,

On behalf of the Board of Directors of the Alaska-Siberia Research Center, I welcome you to the dedication of the World War II Alaska-Siberia Lend-Lease Memorial. The Center began this project nearly 6 years ago. With the help of many individuals, agencies and government organizations we made great progress resulting in this World War II Memorial. This magnificent monument is a permanent reminder to mankind of a remarkable chapter in the world's history, when peace-seeking nations united against evil.

Between 1939 and 1945, in this "worst of times," fifty-five million people died violent deaths; the majority among them died not as soldiers-in-arms but as defenseless civilians, including millions of victims of the Holocaust. Yet, it was also, in some ways, the "best of times," when countries of the world rallied against the ultimate rogue states, Germany and Japan, and when German Nazism and Japanese militarism suffered total defeat.

The United States' Lend-Lease program contributed greatly to the victory of World War II, and the Great Patriotic War in the Soviet Union, in particular. The materials transferred from the United States to the Soviet Union between 1941 to 1945 were

Alexander Dolitsky interprets the features of the Lend-Lease Memorial for Fairbanks resident Nancy Baker (WASP 43-W-4), who is wearing her WASP jacket. Photo: Blake Smith.

indeed staggering: they included, among other items, nearly 15,000 airplanes, 7,000 tanks, 51,000 jeeps, 376,000 trucks, 132,000 machine guns, 4.5 million tons of food supplies, 107 million tons of cotton, and more than 15 million army boots. At its peak in 1944, American help amounted to 12 percent of the Soviet Gross National Product.[4]

During World War II, Fairbanks was a key point for the transfer of nearly 8,000 warplanes from the United States to the Russian Front via the Alaska-Siberia Airway. In the three years of the Airway, thousands of Americans worked with Soviets on the cooperative program. From 1942 to 1945, the Alaska-Siberia Lend-Lease program demonstrated that two nations could set aside differing views, cultural values, and principles to achieve a common, mutually beneficial goal — to defeat Nazi Germany and its Axis powers.

---

[4] Istvan Deak, "Allies and Enemies," *New Republic*, July 3, 2006, p. 35.

The heroism and dedication of the Soviet and American pilots of the Alaska-Siberia Airway will not be forgotten. It is our civic duty to express our deep respect to the World War II veterans. This is our history. Future generations should be brought up with a respectful spirit of patriotism to understand this history of cooperation between our countries. The Alaska-Siberia Lend-Lease Memorial will preserve awareness of that massive effort for all time.

Master of Ceremony John Binkley (second from right) and Program Manager Alexander Dolitsky (right) interpret the features of the WWII Alaska-Siberia Lend-Lease Memorial to the U.S. Defense Secretary Donald H. Rumsfeld (left) and Russian Defense Minister Sergei Ivanov (second from left). Fairbanks, Alaska, August 27th, 2006. Photo: Allan Engstrom.

Alaska's Role in World Peace

Remarks by Loren Leman
Lieutenant Governor of the State of Alaska, Juneau, Alaska
World War II Alaska-Siberia Lend-Lease Memorial Dedication, Fairbanks, Alaska
August 27th, 2006

Ladies and Gentlemen,

Alaska and Russia have had a long historic relationship. Even before Russian explorers spotted Alaska's great land to the east in the 1600s and early 1700s, it is generally accepted that hundreds, even thousands of years earlier, many of Alaska's Native populations migrated from Russia, Mongolia and other parts of Asia to Alaska. The relationship between Russia's aboriginal people, especially in the Russian Far East, and Alaska's Native people is unmistakable. And linguists link their languages.

From the time of resource exploitation, colonization by the Russian-American Company and influence by the Russian Orthodox Church in the late 1700s until Russia sold its interest in Alaska to the United States in 1867, nearly all of the people in Alaska were either of Alaska Native ancestry, were Russian immigrants or were descendents of these. I count my ancestors among these—starting with a marriage in Kodiak in 1798 between Yefim Rastorguev, a Russian shipwright, and an Alutiiq woman from Afognak named Agrafena.

The evidence of Russian influence in Alaska is still noticeable—from religious heritage to place names—and even family names. Minister Ivanov—yours is a very popular family name in Alaska! Maybe you are a cousin!

Following Russia's October Socialist Revolution of 1917, Russian Orthodox influence in Alaska diminished, trade across the Bering Strait declined and the relationship between the new Soviet Union and the United States cooled. However, when Nazi Germany began attacking Russia in 1941, the role of the United States and its Allies became clear. We were not going to stand by without defending freedom—and, of course, when the Japanese attacked us at Pearl Harbor, we were immediately drawn into the war.

Construction of the Alaska Highway to help in defending Alaska became a high priority. The Alaska route for ferrying U.S.-manufactured aircraft really became a natural choice. It is interesting that a few years earlier, in 1935, Army Brigadier General Billy Mitchell had identified Alaska as the central

Lieutenant Governor of the State of Alaska Loren Leman (left) and Master of Ceremony John Binkley (second from right) give Secretary of Defense Donald Rumsfeld and Russian Minister of Defense Sergei Ivanov a tour of the bronze and granite monument at the dedication of the WWII Alaska-Siberia Lend-Lease Memorial in Fairbanks, Alaska, August 27th, 2006. Photo: Sergei Maurits.

place in the world for aircraft operations. Alaska is located near the center of the northern hemisphere. General Mitchell is still correct in his observations.

Alaska's strategic location provides unique opportunities for our involvement in commerce—but, Secretary Rumsfeld, as you hear from your military leaders in Alaska, it also provides unique opportunities for training and military operations in defense of all of North America. And, as you have observed, Alaska provides tremendous community support for our military.

Today the United States, Canada, and the Russian Federation conduct joint training exercises for search and rescue and cooperate on management of fisheries resources in international waters. Alaska is happy to provide training grounds for many of these operations—and assist in saving lives of people beyond our borders.

Ladies and gentlemen, I am grateful that despite our differences during another era, our countries were able to cooperate in defense of the free world. I recognize and honor the men and women who worked hard, and in too many cases gave their lives, supporting this effort to bring peace to our world.

Lieutenant Governor of the State of Alaska Loren Leman speaks during the Alaska-Siberia Lend-Lease Memorial dedication, Fairbanks, Alaska, August 27th, 2006. Courtesy of Fairbanks Daily News-Miner. *Photo: John Hagen.*

History of the Alaska-Siberia Lend-Lease Program

Remarks by Gary Wilken
Alaska State Senator, Fairbanks, Alaska
World War II Alaska-Siberia Lend-Lease Memorial Dedication, Fairbanks, Alaska
August 27th, 2006

Honored guests and veterans, visiting dignitaries, our elected and military leaders, and my fellow Fairbanksans, whom I have the honor to represent — welcome and good afternoon to you all.

I've been asked to provide a bit of history as to why we're here today and it is with great pleasure that I do so. But before I begin, let me say how much I have appreciated and admired Alexander Dolitsky's passion for this project. He, accompanied by Mr. Binkley, came to us some 5 years ago with a grand vision. It was obvious he had done a great deal of work prior to his first visit to the Legislature. And as he talked to us, more and more legislators came to appreciate what he was trying to do and the history he was trying to cement.

So — I don't think there is anyone that is more excited to be here today than you my friend — THANK YOU for your vision and leadership.

A little history if I might... America, of course, had its Pearl Harbor. But just 6 months before December 7, 1941, the Soviet Union had a like attack and it was entitled by the Nazi Germans — *Operation Barbarossa*. *Operation Barbarossa* began on June 22, 1941, when the Axis forces launched a *Blitzkrieg* sneak attack against the U.S.S.R. Nazi Germany and its Axis powers sent 5.5 million soldiers, 3,712 tanks, 193 battle ships, 47,260 guns and mortars and 4,950 of its powerful *Luftwaffe* into the Soviet Union, destroying 4,017

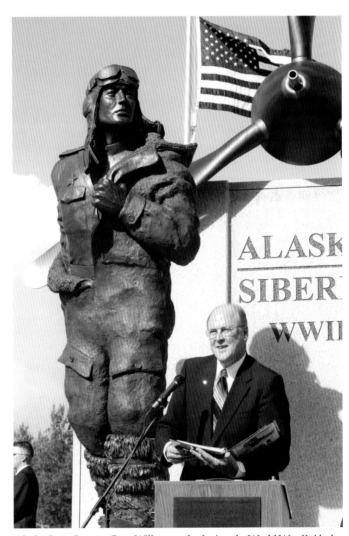

Alaska State Senator Gary Wilken speaks during the World War II Alaska-Siberia Lend-Lease Memorial dedication, Fairbanks, Alaska, August 27th, 2006. Courtesy of Fairbanks Daily News-Miner.

Soviet aircraft within the first week of the war, for the loss of only 150 German aircraft.[5] Within two weeks of hostilities having been launched, the Germans succeeded in almost fatally crippling the largest air force in the world. But the Soviets rebounded and four years later, in May 1945, victorious Soviets marched into Berlin, having won the battle for control on the ground and in the skies.

---

[5] Alexander B. Dolitsky, "The Alaska-Siberia Lend-Lease Program," *Alaska at War, 1941-1945*, ed. Fern Chandonnet. Anchorage, Alaska, 1995, p. 334; Blake W. Smith, *Warplanes to Alaska: the story of a WWII military lifeline to Alaska and Russia through the Canadian wilderness*. Surrey, B. C.: Hancock House Publishers, 1998, p. 18.

While the United States was trying to stay out of the war, its strong sympathies were with the Allies. President Roosevelt had signed the Lend-Lease Act on 11 March 1941, which provided the means for the U.S. to supply war materials to Britain, France and other Allies in their struggle against the Axis powers. And then, ten days after Nazi Germany invaded the Soviet Union, the U.S. Congress proposed additional legislation to include the Soviet Union in the Lend-Lease program.

Initially, all the war fighting equipment was transported in ships across the Atlantic. However, as we all know, the dreaded German U-boats sank many of these transport ships. In fact, 584 warplanes destined for Europe and the Soviet Union ended up on the bottom of the Atlantic and the war planners had to find a different way to move these vital assets to the war front. This urgent need spawned the development of the United States to Alaska/Siberia route and it became known as the ALSIB Airway or Alaska-Siberia Airway.

These were entirely new pathways (or should I say airways) to develop, chart, and maintain. There simply were no established routes from the U.S. to the territory of Alaska and then to Siberia. And just like the Alaska Highway, the Alaska-Siberia Airway had to be surveyed, pioneered, built, and made operational in a very short time, across many times zones of unmapped, uninhabited wilderness, and under extremely daunting physical and mental hardships. The remoteness of the region was illustrated by the length of time it took to locate downed aircraft and their pilots. Some of the crashed Lend-Lease planes were not found until well after the war had ended and, indeed, an A-20 Boston Bomber and its crew remained undiscovered until 1985, more than 40 years after its doomed flight was violently ended by a crash in Siberia. And of course all this work was carried out under great pressure to complete it and complete it soon—the war against the aggressive Nazi army was desperately waiting for these airborne tools.

As an historical aside—the Alaska Highway was being built concurrently with the development of the ALSIB Airway. And as time went on, this new narrow ribbon of road advanced North through the wilderness, and the ALSIB Airways pilots took at least some comfort, not only using the road as a landmark, but as an emergency landing strip.

The aircraft were flown from their points of manufacture all around the United States, to Great Falls, Montana; and history notes, and we do today, often by women pilots. There in Great Falls, the aircraft were winterized and re-tested before heading north to Alaska. They were flown in stages across Canada to Fairbanks where Soviet aviators, many of them experienced combat pilots, trained on the planes before taking off for Nome, across the Bering Strait, and then across Siberia to the war fronts of Eastern Europe where they were so desperately needed. In 1944, nearly 600 Soviet officers and other Soviet personnel were stationed in Nome, Galena and Fairbanks, Alaska, and in Great Falls, Montana.

And this was a dangerous route to fly—the weather and the distances were merciless and challenging. Statistics show there were 75 major and 67 minor accidents between Great Falls and Fairbanks. The Soviets lost 113 aviators in 44 major accidents in Siberia. And in one year alone, 1944, the United States lost 57 American pilots, ground crew, and rescuers affiliated with the Air Bridge program.

In conclusion, in the period between September of 1942 and September of 1945, almost 8,000 airplanes were delivered via Fairbanks to the Eastern War Front. History notes that if it were not for the Alaska-Siberia Airway, many, many of those aircraft would be in watery graves in the Atlantic and the Allied countries would have been deprived of one of their most critical war fighting tools. The Germans, of course, came to know of the Alaska-Siberia Airway, but their stealthy U-Boats and forceful *Luftwaffe* were powerless to do anything about this newly developed and highly successful supply line to the war that was raging in Eastern Europe—a supply line that has taken its place in history as an event that helped change the course of World War II and is today commemorated by this event, your honored presence, and this wonderful monument that claims Fairbanks as its home.

Thank you for the opportunity to speak to you today.

The ALSIB Memorial Honors "The Greatest Generation" of World War II

Remarks by Ted Stevens
United States Senator, Washington D.C.
World War II Alaska-Siberia Lend-Lease Memorial Dedication, Fairbanks, Alaska
August 27th, 2006

Welcome to Secretary of Defense Donald Rumsfeld and our friends from Canada, the United Kingdom, France, and Russia.

This memorial honors "The Greatest Generation," and it is a fitting tribute that the two statues here are pilots. Those who flew the Alaska-Siberia route embodied the spirit of the World War II generation.

In many ways, our countries asked them to achieve the impossible. Together, American and Soviet pilots forged a 10,000 mile-long supply line [from the American factories through Canada and Alaska to the Russian battlefronts]. Completing the mission took real guts. The technology available at the time was not up to the task. The radio navigational aids these pilots relied on were rudimentary at best. Much of the time they had only their own instincts to guide them. They often flew by "dead reckoning" or "celestial navigation."

The planes that flew this route were the A-20, the P-63, the B-25, the P-39, and the C-47. Headwinds in this region can top 200 miles per hour; these planes would have barely been able to make any progress at their cruising speeds.

Extreme weather conditions made the mission even more dangerous. The Alaskan winter of 1942-1943 was the

U.S. Sen. Ted Stevens stands in front of the Alaska-Siberia Lend-Lease statue during a ceremony in Fairbanks, Alaska, on August 27th, 2006. Defense Dept. photo by U.S. Air Force Staff Sgt. D. Myles Cullen.

coldest on record in 25 years, and many of these planes did not have heating systems. Pilots flew in temperatures as low as negative 73 degrees Celsius while peering through frost-covered windows. The conditions were so perilous that eleven support crew died in one day.

Those who flew this route embarked on a strenuous journey. The trek from Great Falls, Montana to Fairbanks could take anywhere from two to twenty-seven days. The mission from Fairbanks to the Soviet Union could last over a month.

Each man who climbed into a cockpit on that airstrip knew he was tempting fate. And yet, had you stood here nearly sixty-four years ago, you might have caught a glimpse of ordinary men doing the extraordinary tasks—charging the runway, taking flight, speeding across the sky, and disappearing beyond the horizon. Their mission lit a beacon of hope in what history now remembers as one of the world's darkest hours.

More than half of the nearly 15,000 aircraft delivered to the Soviet Union [from the United States] during the war were flown through our state. The pilots who delivered them—and those on the ground supporting the mission—were courageous, daring, and committed patriots. This memorial is, indeed, a fitting salute to their service and our World War II generation.

Senator Ted Stevens and veteran of World War II Randy Acord in Fairbanks, Alaska, August 27th, 2006. Courtesy of Fairbanks Daily News-Miner. *Photo: John Hagen.*

The ALSIB Agreement Is Testament to the Cooperation and Unity of Our Nations

Remarks by Rick Findley

Lieutenant General/Deputy Commander, North American Aerospace Defense Command, Canada
World War II Alaska Siberia Lend-Lease Memorial Dedication, Fairbanks, Alaska
August 27th, 2006

Governor Murkowski, Secretary Rumsfeld, Minister Ivanov, Mr. Dolitsky, distinguished guests, honored veterans, ladies and gentlemen, good afternoon.

Thank you for granting me the privilege of giving a few words on this momentous day, as we dedicate the monument honouring those who risked and gave their lives to support the Alaska-Siberia Lend-Lease program.

I personally have flown in the north: Alberta, British Columbia, the Yukon, and Alaska—years after many brave men and women pioneered the way during the Lend-Lease agreement, leaving a legacy of infrastructure and vital navigation aids and airdromes. I have to marvel at their courage and achievement. Minimal supplies, rudimentary communications, dangerous weather, and a daunting terrain—not to mention many parts of the routing that had not yet been mapped out in 1942[6] as nearly 8,000 aircraft[7] started to be ferried here to Ladd Field.

And what a courageous feat it was for our Russian comrades to get into new aircraft, with limited or no understanding

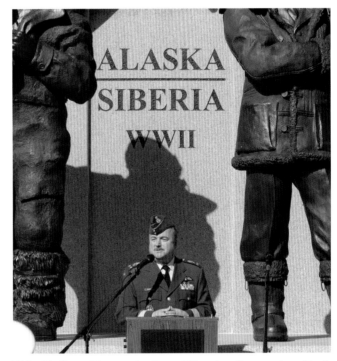

Rick Findley, Lieutenant General/Deputy Commander, North American Aerospace Defense Command speaks at the WWII Alaska-Siberia Lend-Lease Memorial dedication, Fairbanks, Alaska, August 27th, 2006. Defense Dept. photo by U.S. Air Force Staff Sgt. D. Myles Cullen.

of the English language, flying in unknown territory for thousands of miles, knowing their country needed them to bring the aircraft safely to the Eastern Front!

In fact, this agreement is testament to what can be achieved when nations work together and share in a commitment to succeed despite adversity. We salute our veterans for their bravery and celebrate today as the Alaska-Siberia Lend-Lease Memorial is officially dedicated.

Thank you.

---

[6] The first five planes (Douglas A-20 Havocs) destined for the Soviet Union left Gore Field, Montana, on Sept. 1, 1942, and arrived just in time to be thrown into the Soviet offensive at Stalingrad. http://www.missoulian.com/specials/salute/Salute3-espionage.html

[7] "Within a few months, the two air bases at Great Falls were sending 400 fighters, 80 medium bombers, and 15 cargo planes to the Soviets each month." http://www.missoulian.com/specials/salute/Salute3-espionage.html
"Over 5,000, a substantial majority, were fighters, nearly all being Bell aircraft, P-39 Airacobras, or the larger P-63 Kingcobras." "Until June 1943, however, A-20 light bombers had led the list...over 1300" "steady flow of B-25s and C-47s, reaching a total of something over 700 of each"

[8] Ibid., 1942: 2,662 aircraft; 1943: 3164 aircraft; 1944: 2,009 aircraft = 7,835 aircraft total.

"Give us the tools and we will finish the job"

— Winston Churchill, 1941

Remarks by Peter Broom

British Deputy Consul General, San Francisco
World War II Alaska Siberia Lend-Lease Memorial Dedication, Fairbanks, Alaska
August 27th, 2006

Mr. Secretary of Defence, Mr. Minister of Defence, Honoured guests, Ladies and Gentlemen—it is a great privilege and indeed an honour for me to be here in this wonderful city of Fairbanks in the beautiful State of Alaska today for the unveiling of this Second World War Alaska-Siberia Lend-Lease Memorial.

Today, rightly, we are here to listen to the story and to commemorate the massive Lend-Lease support given by the U.S.A. to its Russian Allies. But I hope you will indulge me if I spend a very short time looking also at the Lend-Lease programme that gave my country, and ultimately the rest of Europe, the vital lifeline it needed in the early dark days of World War II when it seemed to most of the world that Nazi tyranny would be triumphant.

Great Britain owes its survival in the Second World War to many causes. A standard list might include the bravery of our Battle of Britain pilots, the leadership of Winston Churchill and indeed the sacrifices of the Russian Army. But there is little doubt that Britain would not have survived at all without the very vital supplies and war materiel provided by the United States under the Lend-Lease programme.

British Deputy Consul General Peter Broom speaks at the World War II Alaska Siberia Lend-Lease Memorial dedication, Fairbanks, Alaska, August 27th, 2006. Courtesy of Fairbanks Daily News-Miner. *Photo: John Hagen.*

At the end of May and the beginning of June 1940, Nazi armies at the French port of Dunkirk cut off the British expeditionary force to Europe and a large number of French Allies. Against all odds, more than 330,000 troops were taken from the Port and beaches and evacuated to England; but all of their arms and equipment were left behind. We had men but nothing for them to fight with. U.S. President Franklin D. Roosevelt, a man of singular vision, determined a course of action to enable the British people, their armed forces and the free European Allies to fight on and survive.

The United States was not at that time involved in the European war—but the farsighted President in a statement to the press to signal his future intentions towards the Europeans said, "If your neighbour's house is on fire and he asks for a hose you don't say give me $15; you say give it back when the fire is out" — the clear implication being that you do not want the fire to spread to your own house. He quickly agreed a deal with British Prime Minister Winston Churchill to supply 40 destroyers to the British Navy in return for access to British bases worldwide. The significance of this was not lost on the Nazis who were desperate to keep the United States out of the war and more immediately out of the Atlantic sea-lanes. This was followed in March of 1941 by HR1776, the Lend-Lease bill, which essentially gave the President the power to lend or lease equipment to any government that the President deemed vital to the defence of the United States.

But President Roosevelt was nothing if not intellectually creative. He decided that it was pointless for his country to send Great Britain supplies if Nazi U-boats sank the ships carrying them. So, typically and controversially, he decided to allow the U.S. Navy greater powers in protecting the ships that carried the materiel; and, accordingly, authorized the expansion of the U.S. Navy's operations in the North Atlantic. This at the very critical time when a hard pressed Royal Navy was trying to deal with not only the U-boat threat to our lifelines but also Nazi surface raiders such as the infamous Bismarck.

Between March 1941 and September 1945, the U.S. spent more than $48 billion supplying my country and also the Soviet Union, France, China, India and others not only with war materiel but also the food and equipment needed by a country to survive in time of war. Of course, there were paybacks—royalties on innovations and bases for lease. Winston Churchill described the Lend-Lease programme as the "…most unsordid act in the history of any nation." It was, of course, to be followed in Europe by the Marshall Plan.

A more recent British observer described the Lend-Lease programme as "…the price of our survival." He continued, "Repayment of debt may be unfashionable these days—but if a debt ever deserved paying it was Lend-Lease."

Honoured Guests, Ladies and Gentleman, Her Majesty's Government will make its final £45 million repayment this year to the U.S. government for its invaluable assistance during those difficult days when we stood alone.

Winston Churchill also said he was a scholar of history because only by looking at the past could we deal with the problems of the future. Today the free world is facing a threat from forces as dark in their distorted ideology as the threat that faced the Allies during World War II. As before, only as Allies working together for a common and just cause will we be able to overcome the contemporary forces of evil that now confront us.

Honoured Guests, Ladies and Gentleman, I thank you for your time.

Allied Solidarity Was Instrumental in Changing the Outcome of the War and the Course of History

Remarks by Frederic Desagneaux
French Consul General, San Francisco
World War II Alaska-Siberia Lend-Lease Memorial Dedication, Fairbanks, Alaska
August 27th, 2006

Secretary of Defence Donald Rumsfeld, Secretary of the Interior Dirk Kempthorne, Defence Minister Sergei Ivanov, U.S. Senator Ted Stevens, Governor Murkowski, distinguished guests, Ladies and Gentlemen,

This is my first visit to Fairbanks and it is a great pleasure for me, and indeed also an honor, to be here today for the dedication of the WWII Alaska-Siberia Lend-Lease Memorial in the great State of Alaska.

Alaska is a land of promise, a land where the pioneer spirit is alive and well, ready to envision bright future prospects; a land where the sense of effort and tenacity can be found in each and every inhabitant.

Alaska and France do share common history. In 1785, King Louis the XVI of France commissioned Admiral Galaup de La Perouse to explore both the southern and northern parts of the Pacific Ocean, with the aim of establishing French settlements in Alaska, in the Philippines and in Kamchatka. Two ships, *La Boussole* and *L'Astrolabe*, set sail from Brest on August 1785, and a year later began a reconnaissance of the

French Consul General Frederic Desagneaux speaks at the Lend-Lease Memorial dedication, Fairbanks, Alaska, August 27th, 2006. Courtesy of Fairbanks Daily News-Miner. Photo: John Hagen.

Alaskan coasts, looking for a safe harbor that could possibly become a trading post.

Overwhelmed by the stunning beauty of Lituya Bay and the majestic landscape that surrounds it, La Perouse dropped anchor on July 3, 1786. But ten days later tragedy struck the expedition; the current carried 21 men surveying the entrance of the bay away and their boats were smashed in the breakers. A cenotaph was erected to the lost sailors on the island, with a plaque bearing their names. The island was named Cenotaph Island, and the two ships left what had been called Port Des François on July 30, 1786.

In the 1860s, many places in the region were given names of the La Perouse expedition. Two mountains were named after the captains of the boats that were lost: Mount Marchainville and Mount Escures.

The French heritage is also evident in the names of Anchorage, derived from the French Ancrage, and Juneau, your capital, named after a Canadian prospector, Joseph Juneau, born in L'Assomption near Montreal, Quebec.

Today, the French community residing in the state is proud and happy to continue this great tradition and to contribute to the progress and prosperity of the community.

Ladies and Gentlemen, France's Ambassador to the United States Jean-David Levitte has asked me to represent him at this ceremony, and I am very honored to do so and to convey his thanks for the invitation and his regrets for not being able to attend.

I do believe that history matters, because we cannot build a better future if we are ignorant of history and its lessons. And it is a privilege to share with you these moments of commemoration of the agreement between the United States and the former Soviet Union that helped achieve Allied victory 61 years ago by allowing the delivery, between 1942 and 1945, of some 8,000 warplanes from continental America to the Russian front.

This very moment is, indeed, a great opportunity to pay tribute to the heroism of the American and Soviet pilots who flew these warplanes under severe weather conditions and at heavy risks, and to all those who participated in this epic endeavour. The memorial that we are dedicating today will bear testimony to their vision and courage during what was a vitally important contribution to the ultimate victory.

I would like to take this opportunity to recall an example of historic cooperation between France and her Allies during the Second World War, one which has several points in common with the event we are commemorating here. I am referring to the cooperation between France and the Soviet Union that led to the creation, in 1941, of the *Normandy-Niemen* fighter group.

As the *Free French* resistance was building, General de Gaulle laid down plans in order to send French pilots to fight the Nazis on the Russian front. In September 1942, the 3rd Fighter Squadron, the *Normandie-Niemen*, was created and sent to the Soviet Union in cooperation with the Soviet Air Force.

From that day, and until May 1945, the *Normandy-Niemen* fighter group carried out 5,240 missions, with more than 300 victories. Ninety-six French pilots will be remembered in history for their glorious contribution; forty-two of them did not return. Today, the legendary *Normandie-Niemen* group remains an example of collaboration between the Allies.

Allied solidarity was instrumental in changing the outcome of the war and the course of history, our history, and our future, in defending our values that were denied by the Nazi regime. Today, as yesterday, the fight for freedom and democracy is still mobilizing us. Extremists and terrorists reject our shared values, the values that have united us since the eighteenth century and form the foundation of democracy in our two nations. Unfortunately, there are many examples to remind us of this reality, such as the horrific plans that were uncovered recently by the governments of the United Kingdom and of Germany.

France, which has also been tragically affected by terrorist activities, is a major Ally of the United States in the fight against terrorism. Our troops are fighting shoulder-to-shoulder in Afghanistan in order to restore security and defeat the leaders of *Al Qaeda*. Our judiciary, our intelligence agencies, our law enforcement forces are cooperating intensively and exchanging crucial information for our security.

Around the world our two countries are resolved to combat intolerance, extremism and poverty. France and the United States are acting together on every front in order to prevent the proliferation of weapons of mass destruction and to find solutions to regional crises. In Africa, in the Balkans, in the Middle East, our two countries share the same goal: to bring peace and stability to regions destroyed by hatred and violence. Our two presidents again reaffirmed our dedication to joint political dialogue and *concertation* when they last met a few weeks ago in Saint Petersburg, Russia, for the G8 summit.

Ladies and Gentlemen, inspired by the heroism of the sacrifice of the pilots engaged in the Alaska-Siberia Lend-Lease program, by the brave men and women who gave their lives for our freedom—and I would like to stress here before you that France will never forget the American heroes who twice saved her during the last century—our countries are focused on the challenges ahead. We are confronted with the same threats. But we are confident and we know that we will win the battles of the present and of the future, thanks to our alliance and friendship.

It will come as a prolongation of our long-lasting solidarity and brotherhood-in-arms that was first forged on the battlefield of Yorktown 225 years ago and was again demonstrated on the beaches of Normandy more than sixty years ago.

I thank you very much.

The ALSIB Airway Experience of Cooperation Is the Most Vivid Lesson for Defenders of Peace, Freedom, and Independence

Speech by Sergei B. Ivanov

Russian Minister of Defense and Deputy of the Russian Government, Moscow, Russia
WWII Alaska-Siberia Lend-Lease Memorial Dedication, Fairbanks, Alaska
August 27th, 2006

Honored Ladies and Gentlemen!

The opening today of this memorial, dedicated to the cooperation of our countries during the Second World War, appears as one more expression of our deep respect and eternal gratitude to that generation, which achieved victory.

The war came to us as a terrible misfortune, a common grief. This pain was suffered and endured by every person, each in his or her own way. After more than six decades, the bitter taste of the losses and suffering has lessened; many episodes have faded from memory.

But that which will not succumb to oblivion is the brotherhood-in-arms and the great alliance of the governments of the anti-Hitler coalition, which defended mankind from the threat of fascist enslavement.

U.S. Defense Secretary Donald H. Rumsfeld speaks with Russian Defense Minister Sergei Ivanov prior to the WWII Alaska-Siberia Lend-Lease ceremony in Fairbanks, Alaska, on August 27th, 2006. Defense Dept. photo by U.S. Air Force Staff Sgt. D. Myles Cullen.

There is no doubt that Allied shipments to the Soviet Union under the Lend-Lease program were a weighty component of the armaments of victory. And it is far from coincidence that this place was chosen for the memorial honoring the great alliance of our governments and peoples.

Besides goods and various materials essential to the front, the United States sent nearly 8,000 combat aircraft from Fairbanks between 1942 and 1945. These aircraft exerted a vital influence on the outcome of the struggle with the Hitlerite invaders in Europe. Absolutely, the Lend-Lease aircraft became the first and most essential of the war material, which began to arrive in the U.S.S.R. from the Allies already at the end of August 1941, and they defended Murmansk and Moscow.

In order to transfer these aircraft from Fairbanks to the Soviet Union, both sides called forth a tremendous number of pilots. Overcoming unbelievable hardship, American and Soviet pilots rounded more than half the globe in flight, in order to deliver their military aircraft by the most difficult of routes, to their final destinations.

During many meetings with Russian veterans, I frequently have had the opportunity to listen to their warm recollections of the glorious events from that time, of the Russian-American brotherhood-in-arms, which was formed under the terms of the struggle against a common enemy.

The march of time is inexorable; witnesses of those events remain fewer and fewer. But the experience of cooperation, acquired during the war years, appears as the most vivid lesson for new generations of defenders of peace, freedom and independence. Such an experience should never be forgotten.

Our sacred duty is to do all, so that the memory of the heroic past never dies. So that obelisks are raised to the glory of the victorious. So that flowers will always blossom on the graves of those heroes. So that our souls will never become calloused, and that in the hearts of our descendants there shall never be extinguished the invisible, warm flame

Gerald Dorsher of Veterans of Foreign Wars of Juneau, Alaska, listens as Russian Defense Minister Sergei Ivanov speaks during the WWII Alaska-Siberia Lend-Lease ceremony in Fairbanks, Alaska, August 27th, 2006. Defense Dept. photo by U.S. Air Force Staff Sgt. D. Myles Cullen.

of gratitude for the military deeds and accomplishments of their forbearers. This is necessary for all of us, for the present as well as future generations.

I am confident that this Memorial will be dear to the hearts and the souls of all to whom it is sacred, including the heroes who vanquished the enemy and achieved the great victory in 1945.

To the eternal memory of those lost in the battle for freedom and independence!

A deep bow of respect to those present, healthy veterans, who forged the victory both on the front lines and on the home front!

Glory to the victorious generation of the Second World War!

Russian Defense Minister Sergei B. Ivanov visits an Alaska Native village on the Chena River, August 28th, 2006. Courtesy of Alexander Dolitsky.

Опыт военного сотрудничества Авиационной Трассы Аляска-Сибирь является ярчайшим примером для новых поколений защитников мира, свободы и независимости

Сергей Б. Иванов

*Выступление Министра Обороны Российской Федерации
на церемонии открытия Мемориала посвященного Ленд-Лизу
Фэрбенкс, Аляска, 27 августа 2006 года*

Уважаемые дамы и господа!

Открываемый сегодня Мемориал, посвященный сотрудничеству наших стран во время Второй мировой войны, является ещё одним выражением нашего глубокого уважения и бесконечной признательности поколению победителей.

Война пришла к нам одним большим горем, одной общей бедой. Эту боль каждый народ выстрадал и пережил по-своему. Более чем за шесть десятилетий притупилась горечь потерь и страданий, стерлись из памяти многие эпизоды.

Но не поддаётся забвению боевое братство и великий союз государств антигитлеровской коалиции, защитивший человечество от угрозы фашистского порабощения.

Не подлежит сомнению и то, что союзные поставки в СССР по ленд-лизу были весомой составляющей оружия Победы. И место для этого памятника великому союзу государств и народов выбрано далеко не случайно.

Не считая товаров и различных материалов, необходимых фронту, из Фэрбанкса с 1942-го по 1945-й год Соединенными Штатами было отправлено около восьми тысяч боевых самолётов, которые оказали существенное влияние на исход борьбы с гитлеровскими захватчиками в Европе.

Именно самолёты стали первой и столь необходимой боевой техникой, которая поступала в СССР от союзников уже с конца августа 1941 года и обороняла Мурманск и Москву.

Для отправки этой техники отсюда в Советский Союз с обеих сторон было привлечено огромное колличество пилотов. Преодолевая невероятные трудности, американские и советские летчики огибали в полёте более половины земного шара, чтобы по труднейшему маршруту доставить боевые самолёты к месту назначения.

В ходе встреч с российскими ветеранами мне часто приходилось слышать их тёплые воспоминания о славных событиях той поры, о российско-американском боевом братстве, которое было сформировано в условиях борьбы с общим врагом.

Время течёт неумолимо, и свидетелей тех событий остаётся всё меньше. Но приобретённый в годы войны опыт сотрудничества является ярчайшим примером для новых поколений защитников мира, свободы и независимости. Такой опыт не должен быть утерян.

И наш священный долг—сделать так, чтобы не угасла память о героическом прошлом. Чтобы росли обелиски во славу победителей. Чтобы всегда цвели цветы на могилах героев. Чтобы не зачерствели наши души. Чтобы не угас в сердцах наших потомков неизримый и тёплый огонь благодарности предкам за их ратные дела и свершения. Это нужно и нам, ныне живущим, и грядущим поколениям.

Уверен, что экспозиция найдёт живой отклик в душах всех тех, для кого священен подвиг героев, одолевших врага и добывших Великую Победу в 45-ом.

Вечная память павшим в боях за свободу и независимость!

Низкий поклон ныне здравствующим ветеранам, ковавшим победу на фронтах и в тылу!

Слава победителям Второй мировой войны!

Russian Minister of Defense Sergei Ivanov speaks during the WWII Alaska-Siberia Lend-Lease Memorial dedication, Fairbanks, Alaska, August 27th, 2006. Courtesy of Fairbanks Daily News-Miner. *Photo: John Hagen.*

Clarity, Unity, Resolve, and Courage Is the Answer to the New Dangers

Speech by Donald H. Rumsfeld

U.S. Secretary of Defense, Washington D.C.
WWII Alaska-Siberia Lend-Lease Memorial Dedication, Fairbanks, Alaska
August 27th, 2006

Thank you, Mr. Chairman, Minister of Defense Sergei Ivanov, Governor Frank Murkowski, members of the diplomatic corps, members of the Alaska Legislature, distinguished guests.

And a special acknowledgement to the President Pro Tempore of the U.S. Senate—Senator Ted Stevens, who served as an aviator during World War II, and who has served our nation with such distinction and dedication in the years since. Ted, it is good to be here in your home state for this important ceremony.

Today we think back to a time when civilization was in peril. And we remember and dedicate a symbol of the cooperation that existed between the United States and the Soviet Union during that critical conflict.

As I was considering this day, I was reminded of a lesson that I learned back in the 1950s. I was a midshipman aboard a U.S. battleship that slipped its moorings and wound up aground on the New Jersey shore.

We thought relief had arrived when a number of tugboats starting pushing at the battleship, trying to free it. The problem

U.S. Defense Secretary Donald H. Rumsfeld speaks in front of the Alaska-Siberia Lend-Lease Memorial during a ceremony in Fairbanks, Alaska, August 27th, 2006. Defense Dept. photo by U.S. Air Force Staff Sgt. D. Myles Cullen.

was, they were not working together. It was only after they organized and worked closely together that they were able to push the battleship free. The lesson I took away back then was that when people pull in different directions, little can be achieved; but when they work together, great things can be accomplished.

Some years later, I was with then-Chief of Naval Operations, Admiral Elmo Zumwalt. I asked him if he had heard of that incident. He replied, "Remember it? I was the navigator!"

So, I asked him if my recollection was about right. And he said, "Yes, that's exactly what happened. Except there's one thing you didn't know. The tide came in." So the lesson really is that it is important to work together, but we also need a little help from the Lord.

During World War II, it was through cooperation that the Allies represented here today were able to defend their people and ultimately prevail over a dangerous common menace. And it was here—in those desperate hours—that our two nations first found common cause. Although in the decades that followed World War II our nations would be at odds, it is here today that we can remember and value the common cause we found and seek to strengthen it once again against another militant and aggressive, fascist-like enemy.

For while there is a legacy of courage and resolve commemorated here in bronze—there is also a lesson—if we are wise and choose to learn it.

In the decades before World War II, warnings about the rise of Nazism went largely unheeded. The overwhelming majority argued that the fascist threat was exaggerated, or that it was someone else's problem. Others repeatedly tried to negotiate a separate peace—even as the enemy increasingly made clear its deadly ambitions. It was, as Churchill put it, a bit like feeding a crocodile, hoping it would eat you last.

Today, another enemy—a different kind of enemy—has made its intentions clear in places like New York, Washington, D.C., London, Madrid, Moscow, and Beslan. But it is clear that a great many have still not learned the danger of ignoring such a gathering threat.

So, we must ask ourselves: Is it realistic to not yet fully understand that vicious extremists cannot be appeased? Have we really not yet learned that no free country can negotiate a separate peace with an extreme and uncompromising enemy? Is it conceivable for so many today to be arguing that the threats we face are simply just law enforcement problems, and not a threat of a different nature requiring all elements of national power to defeat it?

These are the central questions of our time. And we owe it to our people to face them directly. The threats will not go away.

Donald H. Rumsfeld got a first hand look at the U.S. Missile Defense system during his visit to Fort Greely, Alaska when he descended into a silo to view one of ten 54 foot long interceptors currently in place. August 26th, 2006. Defense Dept. photo by U.S. Air Force Staff Sgt. D. Myles Cullen

The only way we will pay proper tribute to the achievements of those we honor here today is if we answer the new dangers we face with the clarity, the unity, the resolve, and the courage that those aviators demonstrated during their service on our nations' behalf. We are the living beneficiaries of their service and their sacrifice—and of their trust.

So, today let us value fully the peace that those who came before us fought to achieve, and pray for the wisdom to rely on their example, and hope that we will face our troubled world as it is, and not as we wish it would be, and that in so doing we will prove worthy of their noble legacy.

Defense Secretary Donald H. Rumsfeld and Captain Jim Binkley aboard the Discovery II, *cruising on the Chena River, Fairbanks, Alaska, August 27th, 2006. Defense Dept. photo by U.S. Air Force Staff Sgt. D. Myles Cullen.*

Defense Secretary Donald H. Rumsfeld meets with World War II veterans at the conclusion of the Alaska-Siberia Lend-Lease program ceremony in Fairbanks, Alaska, August 27th, 2006. Defense Dept. photo by U.S. Air Force Staff Sgt. D. Myles Cullen.

In Memory of "The Greatest Generation"

Remarks by John Binkley
Master of Ceremony and Former Alaskan State Senator, Fairbanks, Alaska
WWII Alaska-Siberia Lend-Lease Memorial Dedication, Fairbanks, Alaska
August 27th, 2006

Ladies and Gentlemen,

A turning point in history is a point at which a very significant change occurs. Sometimes a turning point has immediate repercussions, making its significance obvious to people at the time; sometimes, however, the impact of an event is clear only in retrospect. A turning point can be a personal choice affecting millions; it can be an event or idea with global or local consequences; it can be the life of a single person who inspires or affects other people.

The Alaska-Siberia Lend-Lease program was such an event—a turning point during World War II. Historians credit the Alaska-Siberia Lend-Lease program of WWII with contributing significantly to the Allied victory 61 years ago, yet few people outside the WWII veteran community now remember this bridge between the United States and the former Soviet Union. Nearly 8,000 war airplanes were built in

From left to right: Alaska State Sen. Gary Wilken, U.S. Sen. Ted Stevens, Alaska Gov. Frank Murkowski, Defense Secretary Donald H. Rumsfeld, former Alaska State Senator John Binkley, and Russian Defense Minister Sergei Ivanov cut the ribbon dedicating the Memorial to the Alaska-Siberia Lend-Lease Program in Fairbanks, Alaska, August 27th, 2006. Defense Dept. photo by U.S. Air Force Staff Sgt. D. Myles Cullen.

American factories and delivered to Soviet pilots where they were then flown to the Russian war front. Fairbanks and Nome, Alaska, were the major exchange points for the transfer of these aircraft. There is no doubt that without the American airplanes and the supplies they carried, heroic Soviet pilots would not have achieved the same level of success. An example of the impact of the Lend-Lease program is provided by Soviet legendary air ace Col. Alexander Pokryshkin, who shot down 48 of the 59 enemy planes credited to him using an American-built P-39 Airacobra.

The wartime Lend-Lease Agreement between the United States and the Soviet Union, signed in Washington, D.C. on June 11, 1942, allowed the two countries to provide mutual assistance in fighting a war against aggression. The architects of this hallmark agreement deserve modern day accolades, as do the American and Russian veterans who were a part of carrying it out.

Soviet and American pilots met each other in Alaska during the war, and the friendship and cooperation between the two nations during that period of history is now little remembered in the wake of 45 years of ill will during the Cold War. At a time when our two countries are once again discovering the benefits of mutual cooperation and have begun re-building economic and social bridges, it seems fitting to remind Alaskans and other peace-seeking nations of the Lend-Lease program and Soviet-American cooperation of the 1940s.

In 2000, six years ago, the Alaska-Siberia Research Center proposed to design and to erect the World War II memorial sculptures in Fairbanks and Nome. The time is right for Alaskans to honor a permanent and physical reminder, for residents and visitors alike, of the important role Alaska played in World War II. The World War II Alaska-Siberia Lend-Lease Memorial will honor veterans of that war on both sides of the Bering Sea and re-kindle interest in the historic connections between the peoples of Alaska and Russia.

The Lend-Lease program played a vital part in the defeat of Nazi Germany and its Axis powers during World War II. The Alaska-Siberia Lend-Lease program has also established a tradition of cooperation across the Bering Strait that continues to this day. We believe that the continuing alliance and cooperation between the United States of America, the Russian Federation and the other peace-seeking nations will strengthen and prosper toward the peace in the entire world.

The *Russian/American Summit on Military, Commerce and Energy Cooperation*, with a possible participation of President George W. Bush and President Vladimir Putin, will be a significant step in strengthening Russian-American relations. I am proposing this Summit to be held in Alaska next summer in connection with the *65th Anniversary of the Lend-Lease Agreement between the United States and the Soviet Union* and the *200th Anniversary of the Russian-American Diplomatic Relations* to cement the cooperation between our nations, and to honor the sacrifices made by our fathers and mothers of "The Greatest Generation" during World War II.

WWII Alaska-Siberia Lend-Lease Ribbon Cutting Ceremony, August 27th, 2006, Fairbanks, Alaska. From left to right: Project Manager Alexander Dolitsky, North Pole Mayor Jeff Jacobson, Fairbanks Mayor Steve Thompson, Chick Wallace of FNSB, Alaska Senator Gary Wilken, U.S. Senator Ted Stevens, Alaska Governor Frank Murkowski, U.S. Sec/Def. Donald Rumsfeld; Master of Ceremony John Binkley, Russian Minister of Defence Sergei Ivanov, Russian Ambassador to the United States Yuriy Ushakov, UK Deputy Consul General Peter Broom, French Consul General Frederic Desagneaux, Lt. Governor of the State of Alaska Loren Leman, North American Aerospace Defence Lt. General Eric Findley, and Richard T. Wallen, Sculptor. Courtesy of Fairbanks Daily News-Miner.

Selected Bibliography

Belyakov, Vladimir
    2002   "Russia's Women Top Guns," *Aviation History*, March 2002, pp. 34-40.

Boyd, Alexander
    1977   *The Soviet Air Force Since 1918*. London: Macdonald and Jane's Ltd.

Burns, James MacGregor
    1970   *Roosevelt, the Soldier of Freedom (1940-1945)*. New York.

Carl, Ann B.
    1999   *A WASP Among Eagles: A Woman Military Test Pilot in World War II*. Washington D.C.: Smithsonian Institution Press.

Carr, Edwin Remen
    1946   *Great Falls to Nome: The Inland Air Route to Alaska, 1940-1945*, unpublished dissertation, University of Minnesota.

Catchpole, Brian
    1990   *A Map History of Russia*. London: Butler and Tanner Ltd.

Chechin, Oleg
    1989   "Rescue of a Soviet Navigator," *Soviet Life,* no: 11:39-42.

Churchill, Winston S.
    1960   *The Second World War*. New York: Golden Press.

Cohen, Stan
    1981   *The Forgotten War: A Pictorial History of World War II in Alaska and Northwestern Canada.* Volume 1. Missoula: Pictorial Histories Publishing Company.

    1988   *The Forgotten War: A Pictorial History of World War II in Alaska and Northwestern Canada.* Volume 2. Missoula: Pictorial Histories Publishing Company.

Cole, Jean Hascall
    1992   *Women Pilots of World War II*. Salt Lake City: University of Utah Press.

Cottam, J. Kazimiera
    1997   *Women in Air War: The Eastern Front of World War II.* Nepean, Ontario, Canada: New Military Publishing.

    1998   *Women in War and Resistance: Selected Biographies of Soviet Women Soldiers*. Canada: New Military Publishing.

Craven, Wesley Frank and James Lea Frank, eds.
    1983   *The Army Air Forces in World War II, Services Around the World*, vol. VII. Washington, D.C.: USAF Office of Air Force History, pages 152-172, 448-451.

Datsyuk, B. D.
1970   *Istoriya SSSR* , vol. 2, [History of the USSR, vol. 2]. Moscow: Mysl'.

Dawson, Raymond H.
1959   *The Decision to Aid Russia, 1941*. Chapel Hill: University of North Carolina Press.

Denfeld, D. Colt
1988   *Cold Bay in World War II: Fort Randall and Russian Naval Lend-Lease*. Anchorage, AK: U.S. Army Corps of Engineers.

Dolitsky, Alexander B.
1995   "Alaska-Siberia Lend-Lease Program." In: *Alaska at War*, edited by Fern Chandonnet. Anchorage: Alaska Humanities Forum, pp. 333-341.

2000   "The Alaska-Siberia Lend-Lease Program during World War II" In: *Aspects of Arctic and Sub-Arctic History: Proceedings of the International Congress on the History of the Arctic and Sub-Arctic Region, Reykjavik, 18-21 June 1998*, ed. Ingi Sigurdsson and Jon Skaptason. Reykjavik: University of Iceland Press, pp. 460-474.

Douglas, Deborah G.
1991   *United States Women in Aviation 1940-1985*. Washington DC: Smithsonian Institution.

Francaviglia, Robert
1973   *The Alaska-Siberia Aircraft Ferry Project (1942-1945)*, unpublished manuscript, Juneau: Alaska State Library.

Furler, E.F., Jr.
1984   "Beneath the Midnight Sun," *Air Classics*, vol. 20, no. 3: 25-34.

Granger, Byrd Howell
1991   *On Final Approach: The Women Airforce Service Pilots of World War II*. Scottsdale: Falconer Publishing Company.

Hays, Otis
1990   *Home from Siberia*. College Station: Texas A&M University Press.

1996   *The Alaska-Siberia Connection: The World War II Air Route*. College Station: Texas A&M University Press.

Jones, Robert H.
1969   *The Roads to Russia*. Norman: University of Oklahoma Press.

Jordan, George Racey
1952   *From Major Jordan's Diaries*. New York: Harcourt Brace Jovanovich.

1965   *From Major Jordan's Diaries,* unpublished manuscript, Alaska State Historical Library.

Keil, Sally Van Wagenen
1990   *Those Wonderful Women in Their Flying Machines: The Unknown Heroines of World War II*. Four Directions Press.

Kim, M. R.
  1982   *History of the USSR: The Era of Socialism.* Moscow: Progress Publisher.

Long, Everett A. and Ivan Y. Negenbya
  1992   *Cobras over the Tundra.* Fairbanks: Arktika Publishing.

Lukas, Richard C.
  1970   *Eagles East: The Army Air Forces and the Soviet Union, 1941-1945.* Tallahassee: Florida State University Press.

Merryman, Molly
  1998   *The Rise and Fall of the Women Airforce Service Pilots (WASP) of World War II.* New York: New York University Press.

Ministry of Foreign Affairs of the USSR
  1957   *Correspondence Between the Chairman of the Council of Ministers of the USSR and the Presidents of the USA and the Prime Ministers of Great Britain During the Great Patriotic War of 1941-1945,* Volume Two: *Correspondence with Franklin D. Roosevelt and Harry S. Truman (August 1941-December 1945).* Moscow: Foreign Languages Publishing House.

Moor, Jay H.
  1985   *World War II in Alaska: The Northwest Route. A Bibliography and Guide to Primary Sources.* Alaska Historical Commission Studies in History, no. 175. Anchorage: Alaska Historical Commission.

Negenblya, Ivan E.
  2000   *Alyaska-Sibir: Trassa Muzhestva* (Alaska-Siberia: the Airway of Courage). Yakutsk: Yakutskiy Kray.

  2005   *Alaska-Siberia: Over the Tundra and Taiga.* Bichik: Yakutsk.

Noggle, Anne
  2002   *A Dance With Death: Soviet Airwomen in World War II.* College Station: Texas A&M University Press.

Offner, Arnold A.
  1986   *The Origins of the Second World War.* Florida: Robert E. Krieger Publishing, Inc.

Pennington, Reina
  2002   *Wings, Women, & War: Soviet Airwomen in World War II Combat.* Norman: University Press of Kansas.

Petrov, Pyotr
  1991a   "When We Were Allies," *Soviet Life,* March issue, part I: 42-44.

  1991b   "When We Were Allies," *Soviet Life,* May issue, part II: 18-19.

Poor, Henry Varnum
  1945   *An Artist Sees Alaska.* New York: The Viking Press.

Pospelov, P.N.

    1970   *Istoriya Kommunisticheskoy Partii (1938-1945)*, vol. 5, part 1, [History of the Communist Party of the Soviet Union: 1938-1945]. Moscow: Politicheskaya Literatura.

Samorukova, N. I.

    1966   *Noveishaya Istoriya*, vol. 2, [Recent History, vol. 2]. Moscow: Mysl.

Smith, W. Blake

    1998   *Warplanes to Alaska: The story of a WWII military supply lifeline to Alaska and Russia through the Canadian wilderness.* Surrey, B.C.: Hancock House Publishers, Inc.

    2007   *Wings Over the Wilderness — They Flew the Trail of '42.* Surrey, B.C.: Hancock House Publishers, Inc.

Soskin, A. M.

    1972   *Istoriya KPSS* [History of the Communist Party of the Soviet Union]. Moscow: Politizdat.

van Tuyll, Hubert

    1989   *Feeding the Bear: American Aid to the Soviet Union, 1941-1945.* New York: Greenwood Press.

Williams, Vera S.

    1994   *WASPs: Women Airforce Service Pilots of World War II.* Osceola: Motorbooks International Publishers & Wholesalers.

Zatsarinsky, A.P.

    1967   *Ekonomicheskiye otnosheniya SSSR s Zarubezhnymi stranami, 1917-1967,* [Economic Relations of the U.S.S.R. with Foreign Countries, 1917-1967]. Moscow: Mezhdunarodnyye otnosheniya.

Glossary of Terms and Abbreviations[8]

A-1	Assistant Chief of the Air Staff, Personnel
A-2	Assistant Chief of the Air Staff, Intelligence
A-3	Assistant Chief of the Air Staff, Training
A-4	Assistant Chief of the Air Staff, Supply
A-20	Twin-engine attack or light bomber
A-29	An observation and patrol bomber developed by Lockheed, popularly known as the Hudson.
AAB	Army Air Base
AACS	Army Airways Communications System
AAL	American Airlines
AAF	Army Air Force
AC	Air Corps
ACFC	Air Corps Ferry Command
ADC	Alaska Defense Command
ADD	*Aviatsiya Dalnego Deystviya* (Russian: Long Range Air Arm)
AFB	Air Force Base
AGL	Above Ground Level
ALCAN	Original name for the Alaska Highway built in 1942 via NW Canada.
ALSIB	Acronym for the ALaska-SIBeria airway to the Soviet Union via Montana, Canada, Alaska and Siberia.
AMSIR	American Military Mission to Iran and its home office in D.C.
AR	Army Regulation
ASC	Air Service Command
ASWA	Assistant Secretary of War for Air
ATC	Air Transport Command
AT-6	Single-engine advanced trainer
AUL	Air University Library
AWOL	Absent Without Leave
AWPD	Air War Plans Division
B-17	Four-engine bomber, popularly known as the Flying Fortress
B-24	Four-engine bomber, popularly called the Liberator
B-25	Twin-engine bomber, known as the Mitchell
B-26	Twin-engine bomber, called the Marauder
B-29	Four-engine bomber, known as the Superfortress, which saw extensive service in the Pacific theatre.
B-32	Four-engine bomber, which saw limited service in the Pacific
BARBAROSSA	A code name for the German invasion of the U.S.S.R.
BAZAAR	A code-name for the American survey of air facilities in Siberia. Also the name for the plan, which provided for American air force assistance to the U.S.S.R. in the Pacific.
BOQ	Bachelor Officer Quarters
BOLERO	A code name for the build up of American armed forces in Great Britain.
BOSTON	A British designation for the A-20

---

[8] Modified after Smith, *Warplanes to Alaska*, 1998, pp. 15-16; and after Lukas, *Eagle East*, 1970, pp. 236-237.

BRIG. GEN.	Brigadier General
C-47	Twin-engine military transport version of the DC-3
C-53	Modified version of the DC-3 designed for troop and hospital transport.
C-87	Converted B-24 designed to carry cargo
CAA	Civil Aeronautics Authority or Administration
CAS	Chief of the Air Staff
CAVU	Ceiling And Visibility Unlimited
CBI	China-Burma-India, a theatre of military operation
CFR	Contact Flight Rules
CG	Commanding General
CO	Commanding Officer
CWT	Cold Weather Test
Dalstroy	A powerful organization in the Northeastern territories of the U.S.S.R. that conducted construction operations using predominantly convict labor.
DB-7	Early version of the A-20
DC-3	Commercial designation of the C-47
DOT	Department of Transportation
DS	Department of State
DSS	Division of Soviet Supply
ETA	Estimated Time of Arrival
FEA	Foreign Economic Administration
FC	Ferrying Command
FDR	Franklin D. Roosevelt
FRD	Ferrying Division
FG	Ferrying Group
FLT. ENG.	Flight Engineer
FRANTIC	A code name for shuttle missions to and from the Soviet Union.
F/O	Flight Officer
FORM 1	Airplane Log
GF	Great Falls, Montana
Gulags	Stalin's Labor Camps
GVF	*Grazhdansky Vozdushny Flot* (Soviet Civil Air Fleet)
HQ	Headquarters
HURRICANE	British low-wing fighter; sometimes called the *Hurribomber* when equipped to carry bombs.
IAS	Indicated Air Speed
IFR	Instrument Flight Rules
IFF	Identification Friend or Foe
Il	Ilyushin (Soviet aircraft designer)
I&S	Intelligence and Security
JB	Joint Board
KITTYHAWK	British name for the late model series of the P-40
La	Lavochkin (Soviet aircraft designer)
LAGG	Lavochkin, Gorbunov & Gudkov (Soviet aircraft designers)
Li	Soviet-built copy of the Douglas DC-3 transport plane; there are slight visual differences.
MB	Medium Bomber
MD/LC	Manuscript Division, Library of Congress, Washington D.C.
MIG	Mikoyan and Gurevich (Soviet aircraft designers)

NKVD	*Narodny Kommissariat Vnutrennikh Del* (People's Commissariat of Internal Affairs — Soviet Internal Police associated with secret service; Stalin's Internal Police).
NA	National Archives
NDB	Non-Directional Beacon. Radio navigation during WWII used the ADF or Automatic Direction Finder and the needle of this nav-aid always pointed to the Non-Directional Beacon or NDB.
NR	Northern Route
NWSR	Northwestern Staging Route
O-52	Observation plane, popularly known as the Owl
OLLA	Office of Lend-Lease Administration
OTU	Operational Training Unit
PE-2	Russian twin-engine bomber
P-39	Single-engine fighter known as the Airacobra
P-40	Single-engine fighter known as the Kittyhawk and Tomahawk
P-51	A fast single-engine fighter, popularly called the Mustang
P-63	Single-engine fighter known as the Kingcobra
PAA, Pan Am	Pan American Airways
PBY-5	Twin-engine patrol bomber flying boat, popularly called the Catalina
Pe	Petlyakov (Soviet aircraft designer)
PQ	Designation given to convoys sailing to northern U.S.S.R.
P/O	Pilot Officer
Rad	Radiogram
RAF	Royal Air Force
RCAF	Royal Canadian Air Force
RCMP	Royal Canadian Mounted Police
Recon	Reconnaissance
RON	Remain Over Night
SAF	Soviet Air Force
SCD	Soviet Committee of Defense (Russian GKO)
SE	Single Engine
SHAEF	Supreme Headquarters Allied Expeditionary Forces
SHTURMOVIK	Name for the IL-2, which along with the PE-2 formed the primary equipment of Soviet tactical bomber units during the earliest part of World War II.
S/L	Squadron Leader
SNAFU	Situation Normal All Fouled Up
SPOBS	Special Observer Group, United States Army
SPC	Soviet Purchasing Commission
S&R	Search and Rescue
SPITFIRE	British single-engine fighter, which was one of the finest aircraft used during World War II
TE	Twin Engine
TOMAHAWK	British name applied to the A, B, and C models of the P-40
TM	Technical Manual
Tu	Tupolev (Soviet aircraft designer)
TWA	Trans World Airlines
TAIGA	Boreal Forest
TORCH	A code name for the Allied invasion of North Africa in November of 1942.
U.K.	United Kingdom
USAF/HA	United States Air Force Historical Archives
USSTAF	United States Strategic Air Forces

U.S.S.R.	Union of Soviet Socialist Republics
VELVET	A code name for the plan to place an Anglo-American air force in the Caucasus in 1942.
VFR	Visual Flight Rules
VHF	Very High Frequency
VVS	*Voenno-vozdushnye sily* (Soviet Air Force)
WAC	Women's Army Corps
WAF	Women in the Air Force
WASP	Women Airforce Service Pilots
W/C	Wing Commander
WD	War Department
WDGS	War Department General Staff
WDC	Western Defence Command
WEHRMACHT	German Armed Forces of World War II
WPB	War Production Board
WPD	War Plans Division
WWIRB	World War I Records Branch. This section is combined with the World War II Records Division and called the Modern Military Records Division of the National Archives.
Yak	Yakovlev (Soviet aircraft designer)

Appendix

Articles and images published in the Appendix are reprinted from the 1944 issues of **Bellringer** *magazine, a publication of the Bell Aircraft Company in Buffalo, NY. From October 1942 to September 1945, 2,618 Bell P-39 Airacobras and 2,397 Bell P-63 Kingcobras were ferried from Buffalo, New York, via Montana, Alaska, and Siberia to the Russian battlefronts. Courtesy of the Niagara Aerospace Museum collection, Niagara Falls, NY.*

Another P-39 goes to the Russians as Flight Officer R. S. Berry, USAAF, turns over "The Hopedale Avenger" to Major N. N. Kalninikov of the Red Star Air Force.

A corner of John Stuko's machine shop—constructed from an Airacobra wing box.

It isn't always sub-zero weather in Alaska. Here are E. E. Eicher, Allison; W. C. Wellington, Aero; Edward Freitas, Bell; and Bud Anderson, Allison.

Field Service Representatives Help Speed Airacobras Along the Northern Route to the Russian Battlefronts.

When the United States purchased Alaska from Russia in 1867, only the fishing interests realized the great potentialities of the North Country. Then, more than a quarter of a century later came the Klondike gold rush of '96 and hordes of would-be millionaires poured into the Land of the Yukon.

But eventually the claims began to peter out and Alaska settled down to a more normal existence. Lumber and fishing became its principal enterprises. Once more, to the average American, it became a remote territory, known primarily for its picturesque past.

Now another great trek to the Northland is underway. This time it is a stream of planes — P-39's — following the Northern Route to Russia. And along the way are stationed Bell service representatives to assist the Alaskan Wing of the Air Service Command in expediting delivery of Airacobras to the Red Star Air Force.

Six Bell men are stationed up North. Oldest in point of continued service is Edward Freitas, supervisor of the area, who has been on his present assignment since July, 1942, with one ten-day trip home to confer with Director of Service Arthur L. Fornoff as the only interruption to his stay in the North.

Ed is located at Edmonton, Alberta, but his job of keeping the P-39's moving north takes him to all parts of the territory in all kinds of weather.

There was one week at Watson Lake when Ed and an AAF ground crew worked in temperatures which ranged from ten to 30 degrees below zero. And in order to do their work, they had to clear three feet of snow from a runway 75 feet wide and 2,500 feet long.

But Ed was dressed for the job. Here was his costume: pure wool long winter underwear, a pair of silk hose, a pair of wool hose, fur socks, fur mukluks, woolen pants, a woolen shirt, a woolen sweater, a fur parka, cotton gloves and fur gloves.

That was not an isolated instance of the conditions confronting Bell's representatives on the Northern Route. John Stuko, who has been stationed for a year at Nome, Alaska, the northern terminal of the route, tells of working in outside hangars consisting of tarpaulins and using empty P-39 wing boxes as machine shops with temperatures ranging from 40 below to 10 above.

"The wind sweeps in from the sea," says John, "and makes it colder than it really is. The hotel (by name only) boasts one bath tub which is very popular even though we have to use water from the sea. Drinking water is brought into town from 14 miles up the coast. It is sold at 40 cents a bucket and is well worth the price.

"Food is the tough proposition up here, although it isn't so bad when the boats start coming in about July 1. The store in town runs out of juices, canned fruit and vegetables in December. The restaurant serves reindeer meat—in nine different versions—and storage eggs and spam. You do get canned potatoes with dinner."

There are some compensations in weather conditions, however. When the season brings practically 24 hours of daylight, the service men are able to work all hours of the day and night

February issue, 1944

NORTH COUNTRY

These gentlemen are unidentified but they give excellent preview of what the well-dressed should wear in Alaska.

which is an important factor in the never-ending job of checking the steady stream of P-39's bound for Russia.

"Nothing is thought of checking in a flight of planes at 2:00 A.M.," says John, "and if weather permits, checking them out at four or five o'clock. Among my duties when the planes arrive is to serve as interpreter between the Russians and Americans and to advise them on the service the planes need."

But it is not all work and no play. Fishing and hunting relieve the routine when conditions allow time for such activities. John and two friends brought in a walrus one day.

"We sighted the animal swimming in the sea about a mile off shore," he says. "We thought it was a polar bear. Major (censored), Frank Gillooly and I located two .45 automatics, a .35 automatic loading rifle and a native's rowboat and went out after him. After chasing him up and down the sea for nearly two hours we managed to get within 50 feet of him and found out he was a full-grown walrus, weighing about three-quarters of a ton.

"The walrus started for us while we were debating what to do but luckily, the three of us managed to hit him in the head with the first volley. We towed him to shore with a grappling hook and lifted him out of the water with a block and tackle. We saved the tusks for souvenirs. We donated the walrus to the Eskimos for food."

Ellis (Stub) Hallock, stationed at Edmonton, finds fishing his favorite relaxation. He is quite proud of his record.

"I think I am high man on the fish pool," reports Stub. "I caught a trout the other night which was 42 inches long and weighed 29 pounds and eight

ounces. I hold the pike record with one 41 inches long, weighing 21 pounds.

"Our special bait is made from pieces of salvaged planes, spoons made from stainless steel, with leaders of strands from trim tab cables.

"The big disadvantage in this activity — from one point of view — is that we can work on the line until six o'clock and still have four to five hours of daylight after dinner to fish. It doesn't leave much time to sleep, but who wants to sleep when there are fish of this caliber to be caught?

"We never seem to get sleepy up here, anyway — just tired."

The Bell service representatives on the Northern Route probably do get tired, because their job is a tough grind. Delmer Wheat, who works out of Edmonton, has traveled throughout the area with a special AAF mobile unit and has spent a good many long days — often extending far into the night—instructing ground crews along the way in the service and maintenance of the P-39.

George Werner has spent a year at Fairbanks, Alaska, and he agrees with his partner, Leo Frank, that all the hard work is paid for when "Uncle Joe's pilots are so enthusiastic about the P-39—their only complaint being that they can't get enough of them."

Leo says that the Russians who have shot down german ships with their 'Cobras insist emphatically that the P-39 with its "Poof-poof" (cannon) is more than a match for anything the nazis have to offer.

That's why 40-below-zero weather and hard-to-get food are relatively unimportant to the Bell service representatives in the North Country so long as they can help speed the 'Cobras on their way to war.

Another view of John Stuko's wing box machine shop.

Ellis (Stub) Hallock and his pet bear cub.

February issue, 1944

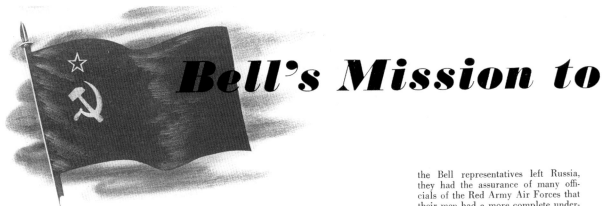

Bell's Mission to

The Russian engineer generously offered to share his lunch with his fellow plane passenger, Leighton Rogers.

"It isn't much," he said, "just some black bread and cheese and salami, but we're lucky to have it. And we'll be eating it for the next ten years after the war while we are rehabilitating Russia. After that — we'll have white bread again."

The plane — an American-built C-47 of the Red Army Air Forces Transport Command — was high over the mountain ranges. Leighton Rogers and his companions — Foreign Service Representatives William Hawkins and Frank Ziombeck and Engineer George Ray — were en route to Moscow on a special assignment for Bell Aircraft.

It was their initial meeting with the matter-of-fact willingness of the people of Russia to get along with the barest necessities of life until not only the war, but the peace as well, had been won. It was an attitude which they were to find, during their four months' stay, was universal throughout the Union of Socialist Soviet Republics.

The purpose of the Bell "Mission to Moscow" was to give Soviet airmen an opportunity to get answers to maintenance and engineering problems on the Airacobra which could be completely clarified only through personal demonstrations and explanations.

The difficulty of securing permission for a visit to the combat areas was overcome by a letter from President Larry Bell to Premier Josef Stalin, pointing out the mutual advantages to the Red Army Air Forces and the builders of the P-39 in such a technical mission. Premier Stalin was quick to realize the value of the suggestion and promptly issued instructions to the Soviet Ambassador in Washington to present an invitation to Bell Aircraft to send technical representatives to Russia.

The purpose of the mission was fully accomplished. Numerous air bases were visited. Many hours were spent with pilots, maintenance men, instructors and technicians in discussions of the 'Cobra. P-39 maintenance films were shown again and again to groups throughout the combat areas. When

the Bell representatives left Russia, they had the assurance of many officials of the Red Army Air Forces that their men had a more complete understanding of the Airacobra than ever before.

And the members of the mission carried away with them a better understanding of what the Russian fliers needed from an airplane for their purposes and they brought back to Bell's Engineering and Service Divisions valuable information on how these needs could be incorporated into the new models of the 'Cobra.

They brought back with them, too, a better understanding of Russia at war. They visited the battlefields. They visited the cities, devastated by the invading nazis. They learned how the Russian civilian lives during wartime, because they lived under the same conditions.

They learned what strict food rationing for civilians can really mean when a nation is fighting for its existence. "They gave us the best they had," seems to be the opinion of the members of the Mission, "and it was better than the average civilian gets; but accustomed as we were to the luxuries of American existence, the adjustments were somewhat difficult to make. Cabbage soup, black bread, fish, and tea, day after day. Hot water one day a week. Room temperatures of about 50 degrees.

On the other hand, when the Bell Mission was in the field with the army, they had good food in plenty. "Over there," they say, "the Army gets the best of everything and well they deserve it."

At a Russian air base, Bell's Mission to Moscow pauses for a moment in the inspection of an Airacobra assigned to the Red Army Air Forces. Left to right: George Ray (Engineering), Francis Ziombeck and William Hawkins (Service) and Leighton Rogers, head of the mission.

March issue, 1944

MOSCOW

Airacobra Technicians Visit the Soviet and Learn Firsthand that Russian Civilians Will Undergo any Hardship to Win the War.

Entertainment, too, is rationed, but only because the Russians use their theatre as an educational and cultural medium and see to it that everyone is able to take advantage of it. Tickets are not sold at theatre box offices. They must be purchased in advance with the permission of the director of the theatre.

Every type of theatrical production is available in Moscow—opera, ballet, operetta, drama, comedies, symphony concerts and even a one-ring circus. In addition, special Army, Navy and Police organizations offer excellent productions.

Athletic activities of all kinds are prevalent in the Park of Culture. Boating is popular. League soccer is well-attended. But, of cafes, night clubs, restaurants and the like, there are none. There is one public restaurant in Moscow.

There are numerous movie houses in Moscow, but films are changed once in several months. American films are few.

Drinks, cigarettes, tobacco, candy and such things are rare. Vodka, which is rationed, sells at six dollars a pint. Cigarettes are rationed. Candy is available only in lieu of sugar for tea when the hotel runs out of the latter scarce delicacy. Bell's representatives depended to a large extent upon the American supply mission not only for their cigarettes but for their soap which is not provided by the hotels.

But, these scarcities are of minor importance to the Russians. War is too close to home. Many of the people with whom the members of the Bell mission talked had friends in Leningrad who had starved to death or who had been killed by the germans. Most of them had relatives who had been killed at the front.

Most of them have one major interest in life — to get the war over with and to start rebuilding the country. They consider the present conflict as an interruption to a long-term program and they want to get back to it.

And rebuilding Russia is a big job. One city which the Bell men visited was once inhabited by some 250,000 people. The city had not been bombarded by artillery. It had undergone little aerial bombardment except for the railroad yards. But it had been burned up and blown up by the german army when they evacuated. Practically every building of any size along the main streets had been completely gutted. The metal had been torn up and shipped to german war factories.

Government buildings, business structures, hospitals and the medical research center had been demolished. The dome had been knocked off the medical center and one wing completely destroyed by fire.

But the inhabitants had returned and were living in dugouts while they were trying to clear up the rubble. Men, women and children were working on the tram lines to provide the city with transportation again. The germans had stolen all the wire from the tram lines and even hauled away a good deal of the rails.

The civilians seem to work 24 hours a day at their self-imposed task of re-

habilitation. Women drive steam rollers and tractors. Groups of women and children can be found at midnight, unloading trucks full of wood which women have cut down in the forests, loaded onto the trucks and driven into the city.

Men of the Red Army told Bell's representatives that they have a deep appreciation for the eagerness of the civilian population to set aside everything for victory and that they feel that it is their job on the front to fulfill the civilian's hope of winning the war as soon as possible.

They told the Bell men that a major factor in Russian victories is the Airacobra. The men who fly them like the climb, speed and firepower of the P-39. They like its ease of handling on the ground and in the air. They like its durability. They say it is a ship which gives them the feeling that it will bring them home.

Bell's "Mission to Moscow" has completed its assignment. But, in Russia, the Airacobra continues to lend its power to the courageous fliers of the Red Army Air Forces in their drive against the nazi invaders.

March issue, 1944

Soviet BOX SCORE

Red Air Force Officials Reveal That Ten Top Russian Airacobra Aces Have Downed 294 Enemy Planes While Flying P-39s.

Prominent in the headlines has been news of the exploits of the Allied ace of aces, Lieutenant Colonel Alexandre Pokryshkin of the Red Air Force, whose official total of enemy planes shot down in combat is 59.

Now it has been revealed by Soviet officials that 48 of the 59 planes were downed while the Russian flier was piloting P-39 Airacobras. The report was contained in a letter written by Lieutenant General L. C. Rudenko, chairman of the Government Purchasing Commission of the Soviet Union, at the direction of the People's Commissar, Anastas Mikoyan, to President Lawrence D. Bell of Bell Aircraft.

General Rudenko also listed the names of nine other Soviet airmen—all Heroes of the USSR and all officers of the famous Guards unit—who have destroyed in combat 20 or more enemy planes while flying 'Cobras.

The outstanding record established by these Russian aces indicates that the airmen of the Soviet have been putting to good use the nearly 5,000 Airacobras which have been delivered to them—about half of all the American planes sent to the Red Air Force to help wage war against the nazis.

The ten Russian aces and their records while flying 'Cobras.

Lieutenant Colonel A. I. Pokryshkin,	48 planes
Captain G. A. Rechkalov	44 planes
Captain N. T. Guliaev	36 planes
Major G. P. Glinka	33 planes
Major B. B. Glinka	26 planes
Captain A. F. Klubov	24 planes
Captain M. S. Komelkov	23 planes
Lieutenant I. I. Babak	21 planes
First Lieutenant A. I. Trud	20 planes
Captain P. N. Komosin	19 planes

and five airplanes credited to the group.

Colonel I. Dzusov, commanding officer of the Guards unit, famous Soviet flying group, describes a victory against nazi airmen to some of his comrades. Left to right: Captain K. Vishnevsky, Lieutenant Colonel Alexandre Pokryshkin, Captain N. Lavitsky, Major G. P. Glinka, Major B. B. Glinka, Colonel Dzusov, Lieutenant I. I. Babak and Captain G. A. Rechkalov.

September issue, 1944

GUARDS Colonel Alexandre Ivanovich Pokryshkin of the Soviet Air Force is known to his comrades as "sky boss."

To the germans of the luftwaffe he's known to be "sudden death."

"Achtung: Pokryshkin! . . . Attention: Pokryshkin!"—the call of warning crackles through the radios of the junkers and messerschmitts as soon as the famous Russian Airacobra ace appears on the scene. It's enough to make the nazi pilots scramble for home. They remember too well his score of 59 german planes—48 of them while flying a P-39.

Pokryshkin was a dangerous enemy to the nazis even before he became a fighter pilot. He used to fly a reconnaissance plane and covered many kilometers over german-held territory in search of objectives for Soviet bombers and Stormoviks. But he dreamed of not only tracking down the enemy but of striking him down.

One day the Soviet scout sighted a large column of nazi motorized infantry. He dived down and strafed the road. The flak was heavy and one of the german shells hit Pokryshkin's engine. His plane caught fire and began to fall. By a tremendous effort the pilot managed to pull out of the tailspin.

But it looked as though the Russian was caught between the horns of a dilemma. If he escaped from burning to death in the plane, capture seemed certain. Dozens of german soldiers were running towards the clearing where they were positive he would have to make a forced landing.

Pokryshkin outwitted them, though. He succeeded in keeping his plane in the air until he reached a nearby hill. He made a pancake landing and disappeared in a thicket.

Two days later, worn out, ragged and badly burned, he turned up at his airdrome. And in a short time he was in the air again, fighting as courageously as ever.

The future ace of aces became a fighter pilot in April 1943 when fierce air battles were in progress over the Kuban. His skill in the air soon made him a squadron leader and his bravery became known far beyond his regiment. He executed every task assigned to him with outstanding courage and with perfect efficiency.

Odds mean nothing to Pokryshkin. He has taken part eagerly in dozens of dog fights and large-scale combats. His success is explained by his courage, his scorn of death and his motto—it's not numbers but skill that counts.

There was the time when five fighters led by Pokryshkin were patrolling over the front line when ten german bombers escorted by 20 messerschmitts appeared in the distance.

"Prepare to attack," Pokryshkin ordered over the radio.

The Soviet fighters climbed and then swooped down on the messerschmitts. As usual, the "sky boss" was leading the attack.

With the sun on his back, he charged at one of the germans and fired his machine guns at short range. The messerschmitt went down in flames.

Sub-Lieutenant Stepanov knocked out another enemy fighter.

A third tried to attack Pokryshkin, but Hero of the Soviet Union Captain Grigori Rechkalov, who himself has downed 44 german planes while flying an Airacobra, came to his commander's aid. He got on the messerschmitt's tail, opened up with everything he had, hit it so hard that the nazi plane fell to pieces in the air.

"Well done," came the commander's voice over the radio. "Nice work."

The combat went on for a long time but finally the remaining german fighters broke under the pressure and fled. The junkers quickly followed suit.

There was another time when ten aircraft led by Pokryshkin met 60 enemy bombers flying in three groups under a fighter escort. The Russian leader decided to attack the numerically superior enemy.

He divided his planes into two groups. One engaged the messerschmitts while the other, with Pokryshkin at the head, went after the bombers. The daring maneuver scored four nazi bombers for the Soviet pilots and forced the others to jettison their bombloads and flee for home.

Then again, there was the time over the Kuban, when Pokryshkin's fighters sighted 50 enemy bombers escorted by ten messerschmitts. The odds were overwhelmingly against the Soviet pilots. To add to their problems their ammunition and fuel had practically run out. They waited anxiously for their commander's decision.

"We will fight," came his calm voice over the radio.

And fight they did. Pokryshkin chose a plan of attack which only the bravest pilots could be expected to carry out. The fighters dispersed and lunged forward. They penetrated inside the enemy formation and began to chase the bombers.

The messerschmitts in their turn went after the Soviet planes. In the melee, the messerschmitts fired machine guns at their own junkers.

Meanwhile Pokryshkin, making good use of the little ammunition that he had, destroyed four german bombers.

Finally, the enemy was compelled to retreat before the practically unarmed Russian fighters.

These combats are typical of Pokryshkin's tactics. The enemy can have numerical and every other advantage, but the Allied ace of aces will take the offensive and win because of his greater skill, resourcefulness and courage.

His gallantry in action brought him the title of Hero of the Soviet Union in May 1943. Three months later the Presidium of the Supreme Soviet of the USSR conferred the second Gold Star Medal on him. Recently he was awarded a third. By government decree a bust of the famous flyer is to be erected in Novosibirsk, his native town.

Included among the decorations he now holds are three Gold Star Medals, two Orders of Lenin, the Order of the Red Banner, the Badge of the Guards and the Distinguished Service Medal from the United States. He has flown more than 550 air missions, fought 140 air battles.

It is easy to understand why Guards Colonel Alexandre Ivanovich Pokryshkin, former Novosibirsk fitter, is affectionately known to his comrades of the air as "sky boss."

Colonel of the Guards Alexandre Pokryshkin of the Soviet Air Force—"Sky Boss."

(Preslit—Sovfoto)

October issue, 1944

Pipe Line TO RUSSIA

'Cobras Flying the Northern Route to Soviet Battlefronts Blaze Air Trails for Future Commerce.
by W. H. SHIPPEN, JR., Aviation Editor, The Washington Star

Wm. H. Shippen, Jr.

Thousands of fighters and bombers flying to R u s s i a through Alaska are blazing an important air route for future commerce.

This military "pipe line," developed in secret for almost two years, may help to win the peace as well as the war by opening our land bridge to Asia to profitable, two-way traffic.

At busy terminals in Alaska, Joe Stalin's boys are getting acquainted with Yankee engineers and technicians, and with the ferry pilots who deliver slugging Airacobras, and their successors, the Kingcobras, along with A-20 attack bombers, hard-hitting B-25s, and reliable two-engined transports.

The Joes from across the Bering Sea and the Yankees talk the same language—sign language, that is. Everybody understood when a big Soviet ace clasped the nose of a new P-63 Kingcobra in his arms, and began to stroke the projecting 37mm cannon. When he spoke a few endearments, the interpreter scarcely had to translate:

"Nize baby. Plenty hot baby—the hitler-ites will love you, no? We have plenty of girls back home, but not nize babies like you. We will get along good together."

Another pilot fresh from the front gave a 'Cobra such an exuberant burst of throttle on the take-off that an American service man said to the interpreter: "Tell him the engine won't last long with all that throttle."

"He says," the interpreter replied, "he may not last long either."

Since September, 1942, the Air Transport Command of the AAF has delivered nearly 5,000 fighters, bombers and transports to the Russians in Alaska. The work of the Alaskan Wing, under command of Brigadier General Dale V. Gaffney, is almost unknown to the general public because of military security restrictions.

New planes are fed into Great Falls, Montana, and ferried north to Ladd Field at Fair-

banks. There they are checked over and accepted by the Russians, who fly them to Nome, across the Bering Sea and down through Siberia to the Russo-german front.

When the Russians last spring were preparing a great offensive timed with the Allied landings across the Channel, more than 360 fully-equipped fighting planes were delivered to Alaska in the month of April alone.

At Ladd Field and at the ATC base at Nome, the men of the two services eat in the same messes, frequent the same post exchanges, attend the same movies, receive treatment in the same hospital wards, and strive with more or less success to learn each other's language.

On Red Army Day, February 23, the Russians entertain, and on American Army Day, April 6, the Americans reciprocate, but not with vodka.

With Russian cooperation, experts say, land routes could branch out through Siberia to Asia and the Rich East Indies. Long hops over the Pacific would be avoided. Winter conditions are no more difficult, pilots say, than those on the Chicago-Seattle route, flown the year round on regular night and day schedules.

The route to Alaska was recommended by a joint United States and Canadian defense commission in November, 1940.

The Canadians began to build fields from Edmonton, present ATC wing headquarters, northward toward Alaska, with Whitehorse, Yukon Territory, as a major base between Edmonton and Fairbanks. Transport time between Great Falls and Nome is now about 17 hours. Construction of the route was speeded when the japs struck at Pearl Harbor, and again when they hit Dutch Harbor in June, 1942.

Planes for Russia were being shipped by boat, especially much-needed fighters. Longer-range types were flown by the long South Atlantic route across Africa and the Middle East to Persian Gulf points.

The distance from Great Falls to Moscow is 7,900 miles. From Miami to Moscow via the Persian Gulf is 13,200 miles. The potential saving in time, fuel, number of ferry pilots required, and wear and tear on engines was obvious.

When an agreement was reached with the Soviet two years ago to deliver planes over the new route, Colonel Alva J. Harvey, one of the ATC's leading round-the-world pilots, took off for Moscow to work out details.

A few weeks later a camouflaged Russian transport and an American-built B-25, both bearing the Red Star of Russia, crossed from Siberia and landed at Fairbanks with the first Russian military mission to Alaska.

General Gaffney, then in command of Ladd Field, had gone north in 1940 to found the AAF Cold Weather Test Detachment. Lessons learned by this unit and by colleagues at Wright Field helped to keep lend-lease planes on the wing winter and summer.

(Official Photo U.S. Air Forces)
Brigadier General Dale V. Gaffney, Alaskan Wing, Air Transport Command, Army Air Forces.

Page Thirty

October issue, 1944

Index

About the Editor

Alexander B. Dolitsky was born and raised in Kiev in the former Soviet Union. He received an M.A. in history from Kiev Pedagogical Institute, Ukraine, in 1976; an M.A. in anthropology and archaeology from Brown University in 1983; and attended the Ph.D. program in anthropology at Bryn Mawr College from 1983 to 1985, where he was also lecturer in the Russian Center. In the U.S.S.R., he was a social studies teacher for three years, and an archaeologist for five years for the Ukranian Academy of Sciences. In 1978, he settled in the United States. Dolitsky visited Alaska for the first time in 1981, while conducting field research for graduate school at Brown. He lived first in Sitka in 1985 and then settled in Juneau in 1986. From 1985 to 1987, he was a U.S. Forest Service archaeologist and social scientist. He was an Adjunct Assistant Professor of Russian Studies at the University of Alaska Southeast from 1985 to 1999; Social Studies Instructor at the Alyeska Central School,

Alaska Department of Education and Yukon-Koyukuk School District from 1988 to 2006; and has been the Director of the Alaska-Siberia Research Center (see www.aksrc.org) from 1990 to present. He has conducted about 30 field studies in various areas of the former Soviet Union (including Siberia), Central Asia, South America, Eastern Europe and the United States (including Alaska). Dolitsky has been a lecturer on the *World Discoverer* and *Spirit of Oceanus* vessels in the Arctic and sub-Arctic regions. He was the Project Manager for the WWII Alaska-Siberia Lend Lease Memorial, which was erected in Fairbanks in 2006. He has published extensively in the fields of anthropology, history, archaeology, and ethnography. His more recent publications include *Fairy Tales and Myths of the Bering Strait Chukchi, Ancient Tales of Kamchatka, Tales and Legends of the Yupik Eskimos of Siberia,* and *Old Russia in Modern America: A Case from Russian Old Believers in Alaska.* He is currently working on a book entitled *Fairy Tales and Myths of the Siberian Tiger.*